The Arrow
And
The Sparrow

Londyn Trotter

Copyright 2023 Londyn Trotter

All rights reserved.

All rights reserved. No part of this publication may be reproduced, distributed, or transmitted in any form or by any means, including photocopying, recording, or other electronic or mechanical methods, without the author's prior written permission, except in the case of brief quotations embodied in critical reviews and certain other non-commercial uses permitted by copyright law. For permission requests, please get in touch with the author.

Contents

Dedication i
Acknowledgments... ii
About the Author iii
Chapter One The Grandparents House 1
Chapter Two Broken Glass.. 10
Chapter Three Cracking Nuts 35
Chapter Four San Quentin Returns 41
Chapter Five Annie 50
Chapter Six Unfortunate One....................................... 54
Chapter Seven Guns and Gorillas 64
Chapter Eight Uncle Pete... 72
Chapter Nine Fire on the Hillside 80
Chapter Ten Awakening 87
Chapter Eleven The Basement..................................... 94
Chapter Twelve SOS... 106
Chapter Thirteen Rescued.. 112
Chapter Fourteen Aunt Betty 119
Chapter Fifteen Goodbye Daddy 126
Chapter Sixteen Magdala... 133
Chapter Seventeen Transitions 141
Chapter Eighteen Passing Through............................ 148
Chapter Nineteen Rebound 157
Chapter Twenty Farmland 164
Chapter Twenty One The Community...................... 174
Chapter Twenty Two Knee Deep 183
Chapter Twenty Three Adam...................................... 192

Chapter Twenty Four Diving In 199
Chapter Twenty Five Shunned 210
Chapter Twenty Six Fun In the Sun 218
Chapter Twenty Seven Trapped 225
Chapter Twenty Eight On the Road Again 235
Chapter Twenty Nine Dead Bones Come to Life 242
Epilogue 251

Dedication

I dedicate this book to my husband, Venton. Thank you for being my forever. And to my children, Mason & Justine— who have overcome many of their own obstacles and are two of the most forgiving, loving, creative humans I know.

Acknowledgments

I didn't fully understand what a large undertaking writing this book would be before traveling through the journey of writing it. I laughed, cried, doubted, and celebrated while writing this story. I want to thank my daughter in-law, Renata, for being a constant source of encouragement concerning my writings. I admire you! Your courage, your heart, and so much more. I also want to thank Marshall Salazar, my project manager. Who carried me through this process, lined all the dots, and was my safety net while I worked on this book.

About the Author

Londyn Trotter was born and raised in the Golden State of California. She considers her faith and family to be most important to her. As a lifelong studier of people, she credits herself for overcoming her own adversities while championing and guiding others to do the same. She holds to a firm belief that your imagination is the wind in the sails of your dreams and that people's obstacles do not ultimately define them.

Chapter One
The Grandparents House

Long ago, there lived an innocent sparrow. She was happy and loved to dance. She pretended to be a ballerina parading across a stage. Side lights guided her strides as she chasséd before her grandparents, father, and two uncles. She locked her audience's eyes with each swirling Pirouette, knowing each one's position. She knew then and always knew where everyone would be. There were invisible name tags that hung from each seat at her grandparents' house. Each seat was eternally assigned to the adults who lived there. The little sparrow did not know that was unusual — she just danced and sang her little birdsong.

In those early days, I was only occasionally aware of the dysfunction that surrounded me. I knew something was off, but I didn't fully understand. I had stomachaches and trouble sleeping. Certain sounds and fabrics felt like a small form of torture. Like the seams of my socks, for example. The darn things felt like sandpaper rubbing my skin raw even when they were turned inside out. I learned to hide my discomfort and my tears like I learned to hide everything else. To this day, one of my last "normal" childhood memories took place outside my preschool classroom. Sitting in a circle on the asphalt singing "The Wheels on the Bus." I remember my auburn haired Irish teacher with her gigantic, kind smile. Her teeth looked so big and white as she smiled from ear to ear while she led us in song. Something about her circle felt happy, fun, and safe. She was like an energetic, loving aunt who showers you with her undying affection.

I remember seeing my grandmother's brown station wagon pull into my school parking lot. I didn't want to leave. I wanted to stay and play. I wanted to stay where it felt safe, fun, and happy. It wasn't a long drive over the bridge, across the river, down the zigzagged road, and past the big red barn into the driveway. This was Dad's house. The grandparents' house. A pit stop. A place providing both supervision of visits with my dad and the ability for my mom to have one less kid in tow.

My grandpa was sitting on the front porch when we pulled into the driveway. There he sat as expected on his old, slightly bent metal chair covered in dents wearing a smile that belonged to him and him alone. My grandpa was not my biological grandfather. As the story goes, he had been good friends with my biological grandpa before he died, which was before I was born. From what I was told, my gentle grandpa assumed responsibility for his dear friend's family soon after his death. My grandpa was a kind soul who was half Native American. He grew up on a reservation, never meeting his Caucasian father. He spoke his native language and English, which I thought was super cool. He also spoke slowly, had a round face with kind eyes, and a soft smile. He greeted me with a quiet "hello" and a nod as I walked into the house behind my grandma.

My grandma was the opposite, besides the 'quiet' part. However, her kind of quiet was different. Even though some people saw my grandpa as "weird" or "eerie." I didn't. I saw him as wonderful. My grandmother, on the other hand, had sharp features, penetrating icy blue eyes, and jet-black hair. She walked with a stoic stride and a habit of piercing her thin lips together. She was a nurse during the time in which nurses wore white garments head-to-toe. A sterile uniform for a sterile lady. Her three boys were all adults, including my dad. All remained inside my grandparents' house.

Only my dad ventured out and lived beyond the grandparent's house for short periods of time. Only to return to his mother's dark nesting hole. A nest would put it too nicely, too pretty. A nest would mean a place of warmth, nurture, and grace. A hole is a space into which you can fall, trapping, keeping, and breaking you to the point of social and mental impairment. It was a dark hole covered in orange shag carpet and 70's Tiffany lookalike lamps fresh from Macy's. Crosses and pictures of Jesus hung from the walls. It looked like an Austin Powers redemption story, but it was far from it.

Mealtime was the same time every day since grandma's retirement. At 7:00 am, my grandmother stood stiffly before her green stove cooking scrambled eggs. I sat alone at the end of a long table, waiting for the usual scrambled eggs with a single slice of buttered toast. Lunch was at noon, and dinner was at 5 Ó clock on the dot. If we weren't there, we didn't eat. If we were there, we ate in silence. I would later understand what my mother meant when she told me neighbors referred to the grandparent's house as the "Munster's House."

My uncle Alvin lived there. He was an interesting fellow. He was tall and lanky with dark hair, a mustache, and a silly expression. My mom referred to him as "retarded" being she was bent toward the use of vulgar terms. She told me my dad had beaten my uncle in the head with a rock until he passed out bleeding. "He's never been the same since Gary bloodied his big head with that rock. He damaged ole Al's head for good," she'd say like she was reading it from the Sunday funnies. Uncle Al played the accordion. To this day, I don't know if he could actually play the instrument or if he just opened and closed the damn thing.

Back to the seating arrangements, my grandparents always sat on the same two-person sofa. To the right of them sat Uncle Al. Next to Uncle Al sat Uncle Pete — my dad's archenemy. Hmm, where to even begin about him? I guess I'll start by sharing with you how my Uncle Pete looked like a little leprechaun to me even when I was a very young child. He was very tiny in stature, had pale white skin, freckles, orange-red hair, walked slumped over, and had a nervous twitch accompanied by a sound between a hiccup and a snort. You might expect the same sound from a skinny, malnourished pig digging in the mud for scraps.

In the middle of the far wall sat a chair that was my father's seat. He, the king, being smarter and more charming than his two dimwitted brothers, sat with his left leg crossed over the other in a manly position, exposing his ankle-high zipped-up leather boots. Deliberately exposing the top of his abalone-shelled pocketknife. Cigarette in hand, he would snatch his silver zippo lighter and light his cigarettes. His emerald green eyes served as his binoculars while he scouted the room for his prey. Even so, I remember thinking he was handsome as a little girl. In the evenings, the ember glow from his cigarettes revealed his smooth olive complexion and perfectly highlighted his eyes. An unexplainable radiance emanated from his skin. He spent his mornings blowing his dark shoulder-length hair dry before finishing with a couple of Aqua Net hair spray blasts. Holding his can of hairspray was my job, a duty that made me feel special in some small way. My dad appeared larger than life when he sat on his orange and white floral oversized chair. A real King Tut. I didn't know then that my grandparents' house would end up being King Tutankhamun's tomb.

As the night would darken and the time would increase, so would my dad's intoxication. A magnum bottle of wine almost emptied. Remnants of a couple of packs of cigs resting inside an amber glass ashtray, the games would begin. The intensity of his scans increased with each cigarette he smashed. A curl at the corner of his mouth would start to rise until his full lips made a full-blown smirk — lips I inherited.

I knew even as a little girl when we were approaching the time when his clever charm would turn to dark humor, and his family would become the target of his evil thoughts and plots, the blunt of his jokes. As a horror flick would begin to play, my grandparents would excuse themselves off to bed. While I would prepare my little heart to brave another storm.

My dance had ended. My song was silenced. Praise of my performance faded into a distant memory. *The sparrow searched for a safe nest inside her grandparents' house. A safe place to brace herself, to prepare herself, to hide herself in plain sight because her wings were not strong enough to help her fly away. No, they were clipped closely to her sides.*

"Pick up and play Al." Gary shouted from his royal recliner. Uncle Al looked drunk and dumbfounded. He staggered to his accordion with a mumbled slur, and with a quick hand-to-mouth, wiped a stream of saliva. He opened and closed the instrument. It was loud, but louder than the sound coming from the keys on the accordion was the heightened pace of my heartbeat.

I could feel the temperature inside the room rise. From his throne, Gary smiled. His eyes were like two green traffic lights that had just been permitted to go, to move across the intersection from silent inspector Gary to condescending drunk Gary.

"Look, Jade," it had started. My dad was pulling me into his game. "See your uncle Al, what do you think?" he questioned with a mischievous grin that sent chills up my spine. Chills so cold they froze my body immovable. What was the right answer? How could I remain daddy's little sparrow and be nice to my uncle at the same time?

"Jade, did you hear me? What do you think? Could your uncle be on tv, huh? Do you hear me? Does he play music good like Johnny?" My dad had passed through the intersection, and I saw where he was going. My little body stiffened; a popsicle stick replaced my spine. "You stay up late at your mom's, don't you? Listening to Johnny play his guitar and sing like a superstar, you stay awake there, you can stay awake here. PLAY IT, LOUDER AL! Jade wants a show."

My dad hated my stepdad. My stepdad was very handsome. He was tall with blue eyes and long black hair. He often wore a bandana folded across his forehead. Most of his friends and "brothers" did too. He was 18 years younger than my mother and had originally been a boyfriend to my older sister, Deborah. In fact, Deborah had a son when she was sixteen by Johnny. She named her son Johnny after his dad. Even though "Big Johnny" left her alone while she was pregnant for our mother. "Little Johnny," as he was called was born with red hair and blue eyes. He looked nothing like my sister or Big Johnny. Which would be the hate-filled ammo my mom would use to claim Little Johnny was not

Big Johnny's son until years later when DNA results proved otherwise.

My stepfather was strong and skilled in martial arts. He was also part of a band of brothers who referred to themselves as "Peckerwoods." He and his band of brothers drifted in and out of prison. They believed they were a supreme race. They walked and talked with a simulated self-confidence. Tied by a bond of lies and ignorance. Even so, Johnny presented calm, relaxed, and collective. Patient with me and good to me. As people came in and out chatting all kinds of nonsense — Johnny would sit and listen. Unlike my dad, there was respect given to Johnny that wasn't forced; it just was. I didn't understand it, but I knew I was special when I was in the role of his stepdaughter.

"Play it Alvin, play it, that's right, get it!" shouted my dad. I began to melt into my spot on my grandparents' long vintage orange couch, which doubled as my bed. It was shoved against the opposite side of the living room from my grandparents' sofa. The seating arrangement, like a small indoor courtyard, allowed its king to have a bird's eye view of everyone in the room. I asked "The Helper" to help me. The helper was my friend, a voice. Sometimes he sounded like me, but he was not me. He was brave, and he always knew what to do. He had enough courage to endure my dad's taunts and my mom's cruelty.

He whispered to me, "Say nothing. Be still. Stay expressionless. Don't cry. Don't smile. Don't comply and don't admit you like Johnny better than him."

"Cat got your tongue Jade? We can go all night?" were the last words I heard my dad say. I laid down and covered myself with a blanket my grandmother had knitted. Eventually, I dozed off listening to the dreadful sounds of slurred words, out-of-tune accordion keys, and the stanch smell of cigarette smoke and soured wine.

The sparrow had dodged an arrow, or had she?

Chapter Two
Broken Glass

"Jade, Jade, wake up, get up. Damn it, Jade, get the hell up! Do you want me to get a pot of cold water? Get up." I opened my eyes to see my mom hovering over me. The smell of soured wine and cigarette smoke still lingered in the air. "We've got to go. Get the hell up." I sat up and locked eyes with my grandpa. He was sitting on his side of the grandparent's sofa, quietly reading a newspaper braced on top of a TV tray. I looked at my mom as she grabbed my shoes and threw them at me. Her green eyes, the color of jade stone, were almost black, matching the circles underneath her eyes. My parents both had the most amazing shades of green eyes. Thus, my name is Jade. "Hurry up," she said again. "Hey, Pay," my mom said to my grandpa. Pay being short for "Paytah." I loved my grandpa. Even his name meant something I thought was neat. Paytah — means "Fire," and Pay — means "He is coming" in the Wintu language. When we were alone, sometimes my grandpa would say, "Fire is coming." He was referring to my dad but had educated me on what his name meant, so it was kinda an inside joke between us.

"Say goodbye to Pay, and let's go." I walked over to my grandpa as my grandma appeared in the room, she was wearing her simple blue cotton robe. She watched as I hugged my grandpa goodbye. He smiled and pulled his white handkerchief out of his pocket while holding up his index finger to indicate he wanted me to wait. He pulled out a handful of pocket change, our typical routine at departure. More quarters than pennies, my heart filled with excitement. I hugged him again and thanked him. I quickly looked at my grandma, feeling my mom's anxiety rise behind me. Her cheeks were hollow, her eyes black, and she was in a hurry — which could only mean one thing. She had been on a run, and there was probably someone waiting inside the car. Someone she didn't bring inside and that someone was probably a man. And since Johnny was currently serving a sentence at San Quentin State Prison, I knew it wasn't my stepdad. I awkwardly hugged my grandma goodbye. She was stiff as usual. She gently patted me on my back and nodded goodbye. There wasn't a word spoken between my mom and my grandma as I walked out the door. I realized it was early because breakfast was at 7 am. I wondered if my grandma was upset about that. I turned as my grandma started to close the front door and locked eyes with my grandpa once again. The smile in his hazel eyes matched the smile streaming across his face as he tilted his head and waved "goodbye."

My mom's white Volvo was idling in my grandparents driveway. I could see the figure of a man sitting in the passenger seat. I wondered why most of these "tough guys" used my mom as a private chauffeur and didn't have big trucks or cool Camaros. I jumped in the backseat. The car was filled with smoke. Only this time, it wasn't cigarette smoke but the smell of what my parents referred to as pot or Mary Jane. I wondered where we were going as the man sitting in the passenger seat turned around to greet me. It was Nick Mills! My heart sank. "Hey there, kiddo, how's old Gary doing?" I felt like crying. My insides were shaken, my body paralyzed. I shrugged my shoulders as my mom sped up the narrow windy road, past the big red barn, and jumped onto the interstate. I was hungry, tired, and my stomach still ached from the night before. I watched the road in front of us as my mom drove wildly. "Nick, am I driving, okay?" "Ya, Wanda, you're doing just fine." That was my mom's name, Wanda, but her friends often called her "Wicked Wanda," which she thought was super cool. I was used to copiloting Wanda, especially late at night when she needed help distinguishing what side of the road oncoming traffic was on. Sometimes that involved 2 am wakeups to assist her in what she called "a run." I didn't fully understand what a run meant. However, I did know what it typically involved. A run would almost always include high levels of paranoia in Wicked Wanda as she soldiered through dark roads and back alleys. It also involved me sitting alone in the car, sometimes for hours, or going into strange houses where Mary Jane was spread out everywhere, and the white powder would be weighed on scales, then lined up on a mirror, just before everyone, minus me snorted it up their nose. Sometimes people would go into the other room or send me to a different room. That was usually when they had special spoons and needles. Sometimes I could hear women screaming, "Just do it! I don't care. Put it in between my toes if you have too. Just Fucking Do it!" I wondered why they were screaming for someone to hurt them with the white powder. The white powder was a drug I wasn't allowed to touch. I was only allowed to help count the "baggies" after they were weighed on scales. I hated the white powder. The white powder was evil, like the wine my dad drank. My mom changed when she met the white powder. She believed it made her stronger, braver, and more powerful.

She loved being in a "special ring" with who she referred to as "Northern Cali's Biggest Drug Lords." My stepdad being an important "Drug Lord," gave her some kind of bizarre clout. My mom said people would do as she said because Johnny was her husband. I wondered how he would do anything from prison. I learned the many men who came around while he was in prison were his friends. Like Nick Mills, but Nick Mills slept in the same bed with my mom. Even I knew that wasn't okay, was it?

Nick Mills had a special hate inside his heart for me. I didn't know why. I tried to be nice. I tried to be quiet. I tried to be good. Yet, he never gave me a smile in return. He just tilted his narrow chin to his chest and glared at me through his dull squinty eyes. Why did he hate me? I wondered to myself.

I felt an emotional shift on the inside of me. At the grandparents' house, I was sad and scared. Yet, I knew my grandparents would keep me alive, but now riding in the car with Wicked Wanda and Nick Mills, I felt all alone and exposed to the evil power of the white powder. I braved up the strength to ask where we were going. "To get Vicki and Lee, Jade. Do you need to know everything?" Maybe I did, I thought to myself, especially since the two adults in the front seat most likely didn't know what time of day it was.

Vicki was my little sister — sweet and delicate, a bit of a tattle tale, but I loved her fully. She had such a natural princess-like demeanor for someone born into hell. It wasn't only her demeanor. Vicki was small, rail thin, with olive skin like our dad, green eyes, and beautiful thick wavy hair. She looked like a child model. Her eyelashes nearly touched her eyebrows, and even they were delicate. If you can imagine delicate Princess Diana like eyelashes on a six-year-old child, that would have been my little Vicki.

Lee was my baby brother, the youngest of six living children. He was my half-brother, son of my stepdad Johnny, and cousin to my sister Deborah's son, Little Johnny. He was four and cute as a button. He was also very thin. Unlike me, who always had a strong short thick stature, according to my mom that is. She often told me I would be "short and fat" like my grandma Drucilla, my dad's militant like mother. She was no taller than 5'2 and carried her weight like a German Linebacker. Lee was the last boy in a tribe of nine children. My mom had given birth to twin boys who died and another son prior to my birth who also lived for only two weeks before he went to heaven. At least my grandma and grandpa at the grandparents' house said he had gone to heaven. Lee had survived, and my mom couldn't be prouder, especially being he was the son of Johnny's, her "old man," only he was years younger than she was. More so because he was next to becoming the next top ringleader of Northern Cali. Additionally, she had also stolen his heart from her beautiful young daughter, which seemed to have put some sort of sick notch on her belt.

Wanda took a hard left onto Orange Avenue and pulled in front of an old victorian-style home. I didn't know who lived there but assumed the home belonged to someone who had been caring for Vicki and Lee. "I'll be right back," exclaimed Wanda. She leaped out of the car, leaving it running, making a mad dash for the front door. The door opened and outran my little sister and brother. I was so happy to see them. I loved them to the moon and back, as I would often tell them. They were both so delicate and cute. Even though they weren't actually that much younger than me, I felt years older than them both.

Vicki wouldn't stay at our dad's home with me. She cried and screamed when our mom tried to leave her at the grandparents' house. Vicki and Lee looked happy and healthy. I don't know who they had stayed with, but I was thankful it appeared to have been safe. The three of us slid around the backseat of the Volva as Wanda took corners like she was competing in a NASCAR race. Eventually, pulling into the parking lot of a motel. This must be where we are staying, I thought to myself.

Since Johnny went to prison, we had been moving from one motel to another, all in the same town, which made no sense to me. If we were staying at a motel, why couldn't we just stay at one? Why move to one on the other side of town or, worse, right down the road? We got out after my mom came to a halting stop and made our way up a steep staircase to the second floor of an aged motel. Inside I was pleasantly surprised to find a large bed in the central room, a small kitchen, and wooden shutters with an adjoining bedroom. It was like the master suite of a fancy hotel, only this was referred to as a "kitchenette," a motel room on a shady strip. Nevertheless, I thought it was cool that I, Vicki, and Lee would have our own room.

We ate some cheerios and decided to go explore outside. We were good at finding trees to climb, paths to the trail, and creeks to wade in. We spent most of our time outside when, weather, and circumstances allowed. Often, I pretended I was the captain of a ship and Vicki and Lee were my mates, sometimes, we were pirates ravaging the seas. It was during our make-believe adventures I experienced the most joy. I loved playing pretend and staying outside as late as possible.

On this particular day, it was extremely hot. The temperature outside hit 108 degrees, and the cloudy motel pool was closed for cleaning. Vicki and Lee got hot after only a few hours of ravaging the red sea. We went inside a motel room filled with cigarette smoke. Nick Mills smoked like my dad. There he sat in the kitchenette on a chair facing the bed in the middle of the room. Smashing his cigarette into an astray only to light another. Wanda was running about and shouting, "You kids lie down, take a nap or something." The room was cooler than outside, not by much, but it did offer a small swamp cooler and shelter from the scorching valley sun and dusty clouds. Me and my siblings laid on the bed before I jumped up and turned the old boxed tv on for us. "Yay, I found a cartoon." Vicki and Lee were happy as they watched the characters jump around. I was happy they were happy. We cuddled up on the bed and watched the bugs bunny show until they fell asleep like two little pups nestled next to their mom — only I wasn't their mom but a sister a few years their senior.

    Nick continued to sit and smoke, occasionally checking his pager. Wanda was in and out. *Not bad,* I thought to myself. We had a television and a bed. There was even a little kitchen with some food. Beat sleeping on the floor, which was frequently our bed, while Wanda was on her escapades. Take away Nick Mills and the white powder, and all would be good, I thought. My brother and sister were sleeping, but I couldn't sleep. The cigarette smoke and the heat made my stomach hurt more. Nick Mills made my head hurt, and Wanda was searching for something, always searching for something.

I decided to go explore on my own. I walked down the stairwell and browsed the motel halls. Then I headed up the strip. I was free to do as I pleased as long as I didn't tell anyone about the white powder or Mary Jane. I also had to be back before it was too dark or until someone noticed. I walked down the busy street sidewalk and spotted a pizza parlor across the street. It smelled so good. I took it in for a minute and just sat with the smell. I wish we had a house, I thought. A house that smelled like pepperoni pizza searing in the oven. A mom like one of those Italian moms I saw cooking pizza and spaghetti on tv. I dreamed about what it would be like to have a home like that as I walked up the street. Then a memory of Grandpa Pay dropping coins into my hand flashed into my mind interrupting my daydream. *I wonder if I have enough money to buy a slice of pizza?* I questioned. Pulling the change out of my pocket, I counted $1.75. Not enough, darn. I felt hungry for something other than cereal or white bread and cheese sandwiches with cheap mayo. I spotted a liquor store, that's it! I'll buy a candy bar and maybe some chips.

I went inside and waved hello to the person standing behind the register. "Well, hello, young lady," replied a burly old man. He had a long beard and was very big, like Santa Claus. He seemed nice. I liked him immediately. I browsed the aisles and found a score bar, my favorite! I then found a small bag of BBQ chips — I had enough. Thank You, Grandpa, I squealed with excitement. Warmth for him came up inside my heart, and I saw his eyes smiling at me.

As I walked down the last aisles towards the checkout, I saw a little souvenir section with gifts. Shot glasses, coffee mugs, and magnets. I saw a tall glass that read, "I ♥ My Mom." Suddenly, I wanted to buy that glass for Wanda. It wasn't often I had money, and I wondered if it might make her happy and feel loved if I bought her a gift with my very own money. I wanted my candy bar and chips. My belly grumbled as I imagined the taste of sweet milk chocolate and toffee touching my tongue. I weighed it out in my mind and slowly walked back down the aisle, back to the chip rack, where I carefully placed the chips back where I had gotten them, and then back to the candy section to return my candy bar. I made a beeline to the glass and made my way to the burly man at the register. "You love your mom, do ya?" he asked with a friendly chuckle. "You're a good kid," he said as he placed the glass inside a paper bag. "Take care now," he shouted as I walked out the door.

I was excited and a little nervous. I wondered if Wanda would love her new gift. Would she sit it up high so she could see it? Would she smile and hug me? Would she feel loved? Would she love me? I hurried back to the motel and up the stairs running straight into the room. Vicki and Lee were still asleep, and Nick was gone from the kitchen. I heard some noise coming from the other side of the closed partitioned shutter doors, I ran to them, "mom, mom," I yelled. I tried to open the doors, but there was a little hook that kept them from opening fully.

"Mom, I have something for you." "Go away, Jade. I'm busy!" "But mom, I have something for you." The door swung open; it was Wicked Wanda pulling up her pants. Nick Mills lay in the bed glaring at me through his squinty little eyes. "Damn it, Jade, you jealous little bitch. You jealous of me and Nick?" She buttoned up her Levi 501's and pulled her belt out of the loops as she launched for me. "I'm gonna beat your ass. You low down dirty rotten snake. Always interrupting me," she yelled with a high pitch hate filled screech. As she plunged forward, I turned and ran towards the door. I knew where this was going, and I didn't want any part of it. I ran as fast as I could out the door. I heard the door lock and a "stay out" lingered behind me.

As I approached the top of the stairwell, my heart began to sink. I took a step down and then another. With each step, a heart-wrenching awareness began to flood my insides. With each declining step, my excitement and joy dissipated. I felt like I was emotionally in sync with the decline of the downward steps. When I got close to the bottom, I saw a large white trash container which triggered a burst of anger throughout my little body. She would never know. She would never know I spent the money grandpa gave me on her, and she would never know I bought her a glass that said I love you mom. I would never tell her I loved her or buy her a gift that said it because I hated her. I hated what she had just done. I wanted to love her and make her smile, but she said I was jealous. Why was I jealous? What was I jealous about, I wondered. I don't care, and I hate her, I hate her, I hate her. Tears streamed down my red cheeks as I made my way to the trash container. It took all my might to lift the heavy metal lid, but I managed to hold it with one hand and throw the paper bag inside the other.

The glass shattered on the bottom of the metal trash container. The sound of the glass breaking sent chills up my spine, tears down my face, and pain through my heart. I sat on the bottom gum-stained step and cried. I hurt so badly inside. I felt so alone. I felt like my heart had been shattered into a million pieces, like the broken glass resting on the bottom of the trash can. *The little Sparrow was hit by the arrow. The arrow struck the little Sparrow's heart right before striking her mind. Two wounds, one force. It was a blunt force blow retained by the little Sparrow's body. The Sparrow rested and made that bottom step her nest until dark.*

I don't know how long I set on that step, but it felt like forever and not long enough all at the same time. People started pulling in and migrating to their rooms, and some of the people scared me. I had a keen sense of people and could typically read them from a mile away. Maybe not everything, but I could feel if they were angry, happy, nice, mean, shady, perverted, crazy, and furthermore. I started getting creepy vibes, but my pride kept me from moving. Would they come for me? Would my mom feel bad and get worried about me? I wanted her to be worried about me. I wanted her to call my name and call me inside. It was dark, and I had been out for a long time. It would make it easier to go back inside. A sense of shame washed over me. I didn't fully realize I was the only one who knew I had returned my candy bar and bag of chips for a gift which would lead to me being called a "Jealous Bitch" by Wicked Wanda. For some reason, it felt like an onlooker knew too. Like someone had witnessed the whole event. I was embarrassed and humiliated. She would never know, I told myself, and as years passed, she never knew. In the end, she would die without knowing.

I would be strong, and I would never tell her. I told myself again. I slowly pulled my eight-year-old body up and took the long hike up the stairs to the room. I felt like I had done something wrong, like I had been punished. I knew I wanted to do something nice, but I had somehow made a mistake. Now I was locked out front of a shady motel room in the dark. I would have to knock on the door and beg to be received inside. I could hear Vicki and Lee, at least they were inside, I thought.

The door flung open, "There you are. Right this way your highness." Nick said with a sway of his hand. Wanda was in the kitchen frying potatoes and didn't even turn around. "Jade, Jade" yelled Vicki and Lee as they ran to me.

"Where were you?" Vicki asked. "She was outside pouting," Wanda yelled. "I was a pirate on a long voyage Vicki and look at the booty I collected." I pulled out my last two dimes and nickel, placing a dime in Vicki's hand, a nickel in Lee's, I left the last dime inside my pocket. "Here, here!" I laughed as I jumped on top of the bed leading the way for playful interaction. "We're going to sail the seven seas," I joyfully shouted. "Climb aboard, climb aboard." Turning time into a game came second nature for me. Either that or it was survival kicking in. Either way, it was a happy place. No matter where we were, we could pretend to be walking through the Amazon Jungle, playing the part of a well-known news journalist, or pretending to be a grocery store clerk. Small drainage ditches would become the vast open sea, and manzanita bushes would mask as a faraway magical forest that produced a special bark we could make coffee with inside our pretend pot of boiling water. The sky was the limit with our imagination.

Our imagination often took the place of the toys other kids possessed, toys we rarely had, and when we did, they would go as fast as they came, except for my toys at the grandparents' house. Everything there stayed the same, even the seating arrangements. I didn't have any children to play pretend with there. At the grandparents' house, if I pretended, I did so quietly, independently. We eventually ate and took baths. My mom was good at keeping us clean. She was always very clean, no matter where we were. Even if it meant her washing our clothes by hand, she would have clean clothes for us to wear. During her marriage to Johnny, obtaining clothing wasn't typically a problem. Random people would drop by and write a list of our sizes and what we wanted. I wanted the new cabbage patch doll that came with adoption papers and new shirts with unicorns. My mom wanted some new Levis and a pair of Birkenstock's size 7, please. The person or people would leave and return with items from our list in exchange for the white powder. I understood they were stealing our new clothes and toys, but my mom said she paid for them. Something inside me said it was wrong, but I was so happy to have a new possession I stuffed the brewed deceit I felt.

I understand now it was the helper who was whispering to my young spirit, "Jade, I'm happy you have new clothes and a new doll, but this isn't the right way to gain them. Enjoy them but know this is NOT your way." After my bath, I put on one of my grandpa's oversized white cotton tees. The t-shirt still smelled like him. I had new undies, which had been delivered while I ate my fried potatoes and pork chop. I had new PJs, but I wanted to wear my grandpa's t-shirt, which fit me like a dress. My mom had put Vicki and Lee to sleep in the little makeshift room while I was in the bath. I came out to find my mom and Nick sitting at the little table. I jumped onto the motel room bed. The tv was on but playing something boring. I jumped up in hopes of finding something I would like.

Nick Mills also jumped up, meeting me in front of the television cabinet. He hit the power button. "Get in bed," he said. I didn't understand why because it was summer and why was I sleeping in the main room and Vicki and Lee in the other room. Where were Wanda and Nick going to sleep? Maybe they weren't going to sleep, I thought. That wouldn't have been that uncommon. However, the noise was often on all night. Either the tv, music, or people talking until the sun rose, even during school months. "Get in bed, Jade, now," Nick demanded. "I want to sleep with Vicki and Lee," I said. "You're gonna sleep where we tell ya," he replied. "No, I'm sleeping with my brother and sister." I started walking towards the double doors when I felt Nick grab the back of my collar, and in one sweeping swoop, I was thrown onto the bed. I felt terrified but not terrified enough to yell, "No, I want to sleep with Vicki and Lee," I said under my breath before I was hit with adrenaline.

"I hate you! I hate you both," I decided to yell. I was scared inside, but I was also ready to take them on by letting out the hurt which I had endured that day. I wanted to tell my mom, I bought you a present that is now in the big white trash can instead of buying something for myself because I wanted to make you happy, but you hurt me, and you didn't care, and you left me outside, and you had sex with Nick, and you hate me, and I don't know why when I just want to love you and be loved by you. "You hate me, huh, you disrespectful cunt! You're just like your dad," my mom said, standing up and joining forces with Nick. "I hate you both. I wish you would die," I yelled. "My dad is better than you," I screamed. Hoping it would hurt them and inflict just a portion of the pain I felt. Nick's hand flung across my face spinning my head to one side. I heard ringing in my ear, and my cheek felt like it was on fire. Before I could turn my face back around, he hit me again. This time my lip opened, and the taste of blood filled my mouth. I screamed and cried. "I surrender. I'm sorry. I'm sorry," but it was too late. He grabbed a fist full of my hair and threw me towards the headboard.

"Wanda get me some rags," he demanded. I screamed and shouted, "I'm sorry. No, don't. Please stop. Please!" He sat on top of me as I felt another blow to my face and another. Then he wrapped his hands around my throat and through a whisper said, "Shut your mouth, you little cunt, you're about to meet your maker." My mom handed him some rags.

With one hand wrapped around my neck, he used the other to stuff the rags down my throat. I panicked. I felt like I couldn't breathe. I couldn't move because he was on top of me, he was heavy. *Help, Help*, I tried to scream, but only a screech came out. I looked for my mom only to see her standing near the door with an evil smile on her face. Her black eyes met mine, she said, "How do you feel about me now?" She looked like she had just received the gift I tried to give her earlier in the day, or at least how I imagined she would look, but I was the gift. My body being beaten was the gift. I was in a complete panic and felt like I was going to die. Nick was so heavy I couldn't move. I could only take in short inhalations of air through my nose because I was hyperventilating.

Just as I felt I couldn't take it anymore, there was a loud banging on the door. I heard from the other side a woman shout — "leave that child alone. I called the cops, and they're on their way." Then there was silence. Nick pulled me by my hair to position me upright. "Do you think she called the cops, Nick?" my mom asked as I pulled the rags out of my mouth and took a deep breath in, only to nearly drown in my own blood. Which was flowing from my nose and broken lips. She pounded on the door again, "The cops are coming, leave that child alone." "Mind your own business," my mom shouted. "Nick, get your stuff, let's get out of here. You happy now, Jade," my mom asked as I observed drops of blood on my grandpa's t-shirt.

My head felt swollen, and it was hard to hear. My face hurt like it had been slammed into a car door. The helper had sent someone to help me. Nick and Wanda ran throughout the motel room, throwing drugs and clothes into bags and making their way back and forth down the steep steps a few times before we were all loaded up into the Volvo. It was dark, and there was a slight chill in the air even though it was still hot outside. Vicki and Lee were half asleep. *How were they able to sleep*? I wondered. I never could sleep like them through it all. My mom jumped in the driver's seat and began to speed around the cloudy closed pool when lights started flashing behind us.

"Shit, cops, shit." I sat cuddled up next to the Volvo's backseat door. The cops were bad. I knew cops were bad, and they were here because of me. My mom stopped the car as an officer approached her window. "Turn off your car, Ma'am," he said, asking for her driver's license and registration. "What's going on? Why are you pulling me over? You have to have a good reason, you know," snapped my mom. The officer flashed his light on Nick and then Vicki and Lee until landing on me. "We received a complaint of a disturbance Ma'am." "Lots of people here at this motel." Wanda said. "Are there a lot of people here who drive a 1985 White Volvo 240 Wagon, Ma'am?" Just then, more cops pulled into the parking lot. The officer stepped away only to quickly return with more officers. There were two positioned on each side of the vehicle.

"Step out of the car Ma'am" the officer said as an officer on the passenger side told Nick to put his hands in the air and step out of the vehicle. The officers separated Nick and my mom. The first officer came to my side and opened the door. "Hi," he said. He shined his light on my bloody t-shirt and asked me what had happened. I went silent. I was scared. *Would they take my mom to prison too*, I wondered? *Where would I go? My mom wasn't all bad*, I thought. *It's the white powder*, I thought. Even though she wasn't the best mom or a loving mom, I knew her. When the men were gone, and she wasn't on the white powder, we would bake together.

She was from the South and could cook the best drop biscuits and gravy and homemade desserts. She'd bake cookies from persimmons picked right off a tree and she could prepare a potato a hundred different ways. She would let me create chores for me and my siblings and build forts right in the living room when we had a home.

"Hey, what happened?" the officer asked as he draped a jacket over me. I realized it was his jacket. He gently pulled me out of the car and sat me on the seat of his police car. He squatted down next to me. "What happened?" I looked over his shoulder and saw an officer pull a gun from the Volvo and place it on top of the hood. Handcuffs were placed on Nick, and he was pushed over a police car. He didn't seem so scary now, but I was still scared. I knew even worse than anything was a person who sent someone to jail or talked to cops. "Sweetheart, did that man do this to you, or was it your mom?" The officer was so nice. I felt a warmth come from him, but my swollen lips and fear wouldn't allow me to speak. "I want to help you," he said. I believed him. I wondered if Wanda and Nick went to jail, was there a chance me, Vicki, and Lee could go home with him. I bet he had a nice wife and a nice home. He didn't seem bad, he was big and loving, he was safe, and he was attempting to offer me some form of freedom from Wanda, but inside I felt locked up, imprisoned, and frozen. "Did he do this to you?" he asked again. I shook my head up and down. "I'm going to ask you an important question," he said. "Do you want to stay with your mom, or do you want to go somewhere else? Nick is going to jail for what he did, and now I need to know if it's safe for you to stay with your mom. Can you tell me if you will be safe or not? You don't have to be afraid of her if you tell me you want to go somewhere else." *But where would I go?* I wondered again.

I saw the officer who was looking through the car pull out the white powder rolled in duct taped balls and place them on the hood, along with Mary Jane stuffed inside baggies, scales, and other paraphernalia. Nick was placed in the backseat of a police car. He was going away. Inside I was happy but terrified at what I had done. I didn't want to leave Vicki and Lee and wondered if Wicked Wanda would be nicer (the nicer Wanda) with Nick Mills gone, but I feared the backlash of the police taking Nick away. Even worse, I feared the repercussions of the white powder, the money, and the Mary Jane being confiscated. The things that were more important to my mom than me.

"Jade, do you want to stay with your mom, or do you want to come with me?" asked the officer. "I want to stay with my mom," I choked out. "You sure," the gentle giant asked again. I really wanted to stay right there with him, covered in his nice jacket. He seemed like a dream, a loving light inside a deep dark tunnel of despair. Deep inside, I knew the truth. I knew he wouldn't take me and my siblings with him to his home, and I knew what he meant when he asked if I wanted to go with him.

I had gone with a police officer once before when my dad got drunk and locked me outside his apartment before moving back to the grandparents' house. I went to the police station dressed in my princess Halloween costume. My dad and I were supposed to go trick or treating together that night, but instead, I ended up inside a lady's home whom I had never met. She was my dad's neighbor. She saw me crying at the door, knocking and trying to get in, but my dad was screaming from the inside, "Y'all aren't taking me." "Dad, it's me," I shouted, but he thought I was a government official coming to take him back to war. He had PTSD from the Vietnam War, which induced paranoia enhanced by LSD and other psychedelics he experimented with. Later he would tell me he had taken so many telling reality from non-reality became a challenge for him. He would spontaneously "fry" like he had taken a tab of acid but hadn't. His paranoia and his genetics led him to his favorite drug of choice — alcohol.

The lady, his neighbor, was nice. I remember she was large and had several cats wandering around inside her apartment. My parents hated cats, so I didn't know much about them. I had only heard old wives' tales like "cats suck the breath from newborn babies because they smell the milk" or "cats carry diseases and are sneaky like rats." Even so, the lady was nice. She kept saying, "It's going to be okay sweet girl," and gave me a capri sun juice. Eventually, an officer arrived, then more followed. When I left with an officer, I could see other officers trying to get into my dad's apartment. I ended up on a cold seat at the police station until another nice lady came to take me to another home. This was a child protective service worker.

There I was in my princess costume, empty bag in hand, in the back of a stranger's car on my way to a home I did not know. Worse than that were the slamming door to my expectations and hopes which had existed for that night. That door was shut, and a new door had opened. I was eventually taken to an older lady's home; her name was Kris – short for Kristine. She welcomed me into her home and showed me what would be my new room for a while. She had a granddaughter who also lived with her and was my age—her name was Sophia. Sophia was beautiful. She told me she was Mexican and could speak Spanish. I was happy she was there, but I still felt displaced. I didn't know these people. Everything felt awkward.

I felt like a stranger in someone's house where I was going to stay for how long I didn't know. Although I was young, I knew I didn't belong there. I shared a room with Sophia which made my stay bearable. We had twin beds and matching purple bedspreads with matching pillowcases. They were satin and felt so wonderful. I promised myself that someday when I grew up and had my own house, I would have a bed full of satin. I closed my eyes and dreamed of satin sheets, satin pajamas, and a satin robe. It was pretty and safe with Kris and Sophia, but I couldn't shake the heavy feeling of a crushed spirit and the awkwardness of not knowing how to belong where I had never been. At night Sophia would teach me how to count in Spanish. I liked her a lot, she shared with me that her mom did drugs, too, and that was why she lived with her grandma. It was at night when Sophia and I laid next to each other in our satin covered twin beds that I felt like I belonged, just for those brief moments before we would fall asleep and wake to a new day. Then one day, the CPS lady came and said it was time for me to go back with my mom. After that, my dad had to move back to the grandparents' house in order to visit me.

"Okay, Jade, let's go, " said the nice officer. He walked me towards the Volvo. It felt like we were in slow motion. A new fear increased inside me with each step I took. Only this felt like partial fear paralysis. I felt one part of adrenaline combined with stinging lips and a pounding head and one part numb. As I approached the car, the police car, which contained Nick Mills in the backseat, sped away, followed by two more police cars. The nice officer helped me get in the backseat of the Volvo before closing the door and having a stern talk with my mom. I knew her new submissive demeanor was a cover to save herself. I knew the minute the officer left, there would be hell to pay, but it would be better than leaving Vicki and Lee and going to a stranger's house again. Later I would learn the police confiscated six 8-balls of meth, 168 grams of pot, and a .357 magnum revolver which Nick took the blame for. He was also charged with child abuse and child endangerment. My mom said it was because he knew he would have been killed if he had allowed her to take the fall. Even though she got off the hook when it came to the law, she had just lost her drugs and most of her money. Looking back now, I wonder how they even let her go. That night did not end well. There was no "I'm sorry kids or are you kids okay?" There were no hugs or kisses — just a mad woman behind the wheel of her car trying to figure out her next move.

Vicki moved closer to me and laid her little head on my arm, falling fast asleep. I was still wearing my grandpa's bloody t-shirt. "Are you happy now, Jade? You got what you wanted," was the last thing I remember my mom saying before I, too, closed my eyes and drifted into sleep.

The sparrow had survived a tumultuous storm. She was wounded and felt powerless, but she survived.

Chapter Three
Cracking Nuts

Dusk had turned to dawn. I could see the sun coming up but was still unclear where we were going, but as rows of tall walnut trees emerged, I knew we were headed to my grandma's. This grandma had been born in Arkansas and lived in a Big Red House in a little country town. Her name was Georgia Roselyn Stewart. Georgia was about 5 foot one and weighed approximately 105 pounds. She had given birth to six children, including my twin uncles Russell and Rutherford. She had lived alone for many years. My grandfather passed away before I was born, and she never remarried. Wanda was her youngest child.

Grandma Georgia was a Christian woman who loved God and was as corky as a woman from the South could be. Tomatoes were tomaters, and potatoes were pronounced potaters. She could say them, but she couldn't cook them like my mom to save her life. I loved Grandma Georgia, and I knew I was about to get dropped off there because of what had happened with Nick Mills. As soon as I saw the familiar walnut trees, I had the feeling I was going to have a long stay with Grandma Georgia. My mom had driven several hundred miles to rid herself of her trouble, me.

While I loved my Grandma Georgia, she had some really interesting quirks. For example, she would go on food kicks. She would read something that was healthy, and that's all she would buy. We would have an avocado week, a chicken leg week, we would have an all-you-can-eat raw honey week, Lima beans and butter week, and we would even eat popcorn individually dipped in gobs of butter because butter was good for you that week. My Grandma Georgia was the opposite of my mom in every way. She was a bit prudish even though she had six children. She never allowed television into her house, and she forbade the use of makeup. However, Grandma Georgia did like to fancy herself with nice hats, and wigs, she always wore a brooch, adorned herself with polyester from head to toe, and wore knee-high leather boots come rain or shine.

One thing that always seemed strange to me about Grandma Georgia is the fact that when she was in her early 40s, she had fallen off a porch and broke a hip, but she didn't believe in going to modern doctors, so she let it heal naturally. As a result, one leg was approximately 3 inches shorter than the other leg, and she had severe digestive issues. Instead of going to the surgeons to have her hip fixed and operated on — cured and remedied, Grandma Georgia opted to use a pair of crutches every day of her life until the day she died.

Additionally, she would buy her knee-high leather boots, and she would saw one of the hills right off the bottom so that her legs would be the same height. I always thought it was funny watching Grandma Georgia hobble on her crutches down the sidewalk. Her fancy polyester pants were a bit longer than they should have been but just short enough to reveal her uneven boot heels. My grandma loved nuts like she loved the sunshine. No matter what her food phase was at the time, she always had nuts. We spent sunny days in that little country town, walking on the sidewalks, searching for and collecting walnuts to take inside and crack with her nutcrackers. I thought it was so much fun.

It was so different being with Grandma Georgia than being with my mom or at the grandparents' house. Even though Grandma Georgia had her quirks, she was loving, safe, and soft. We had a wonderful routine I loved which involved walking to her chiropractor. Afterward, we'd stop at the local health food store where I would get yogurt when yogurt had creamy plain yogurt on the top and fresh fruit on the bottom—I just loved mixing it all together—it was so good, and a handful of honey sesame seed candies to go. Then we would walk to a park that was shielded by gigantic oak trees that provided an enormous amount of shade over the little park. There wasn't much to play on there, but there was a tall slide, and oh, how I enjoyed that slide. I would climb to the top and slide down as fast as I could, frontwards, backwards, and sometimes even sideways.

Grandma Georgia had an old red house with a big porch that wrapped all the way around from the front to the back. Towards the backside of the porch, it was enclosed with screen windows to keep the mosquitoes and the flies out. Inside there was an old wash basin and an even older wash machine. I thought that the wash basin was so fun. Grandma Georgia would let me climb inside, filling it with water and a sprinkle of dish soap, adding to the fun. I would splish splash for hours inside that old wash basin. I'd help Grandma hang up clothes on her clothesline even though I couldn't quite reach it. I did my best to straighten the clothes and have them ready in hand to give to her. There was something about the experience that felt free to me. Outside underneath the walnut and oak trees, the summer breeze sweeping through the air.

In the evening after we had eaten whatever the craze of the week was — Grandma would rock me on her lap in her rocking chair. Surrounded by heating pads and books, she would sing songs to me while she gently rubbed my back. I especially liked when she would sing "*Old Susanna*" and "*You Are My Sunshine.*" She would often sing a song that went a little bit like this, "*Sugar in the morning, sugar in the evening, sugar at supper time, won't you be my sugar, and love me all the time.*" Grandma Georgia classically closed our night by tucking me into bed and reading me a Bible story before saying a goodnight prayer. It was quiet at Grandma Georgia's, so quiet. But I liked it, and I liked the quiet.

That summer, I turned nine years old. Just me and Grandma in her big red house. Summer was filled with homemade salt dough, lima beans with butter, walks to the park, and a whole lot of Georgia's singing. We cracked walnuts after we collected them off sidewalks and ate them together like two little birds eating off a birdhouse full of seeds. It was just me and my Georgia. Those summer nights captured the sounds of crickets instead of blaring music or even worse — out-of-tune accordion keys.

Late one evening, I remember nestling my body into Grandma's as she squeezed me on her rocking chair. My heart content, my soul at peace. The hurt was distant, removed by location. I tried to push out the fact that Wanda would eventually show up and steal my serenity. Rob me of my safety and take away from me the comfort I found in Georgia's arms, but something inside my heart felt strange. I had a feeling of displacement inside of me I couldn't shake. I could feel pain in my chest when I thought of Wanda, Vicki, and Lee. There was a place inside me that couldn't escape the hurt. I missed them. I hated it, but I did. Why can't my mom just love me? Why does she hate me? Why am I so bad? What can I do better? Are Vicki and Lee okay? Are they alive? No matter how hard I tried, questions like these would seep through my mind. I fought to push them far from me, but my efforts often returned void. I turned to action, to fun, to play once again for my hiding place. Georgia's compliments became the air I breathed, and even though I inhaled each of them, I couldn't run from Wanda, from the love I craved from her. There was something only she could give to me, but would she? Would she ever?

It was late in the evening one Sunday when we heard a knock at the door, "Mom, mom, you in there?" It was Wanda. She had come to collect me for the new school year. I would be entering the fourth grade at a new school — Sycamore Elementary. Something inside me jumped when I heard Wanda's voice, it had been so long. I hadn't heard from her since the morning she dropped me off. I felt a combination of anxiety and happiness. I wanted to see her, but I was super nervous about that door opening.

Our reunion was short-lived. Wanda came inside, looked at me, told me to get my stuff, and started complaining to Georgia about her starter going out. She looked better than when I saw her last. Her blonde hair had grown and was parted perfectly down the middle. She had gained weight and had makeup on. My mom looked pretty. I gathered my things and said goodbye to Georgia. "Remember, I love you, Jade," she said as we walked out the door. "Bye Grandma, I love you too. Thank you. I'll miss you," I replied.

It was time for the Sparrow to leave the warmth of Georgia's rustic nest and fly North with Wicked Wanda.

Chapter Four
San Quentin Returns

The drive back to our hometown was awkward and slightly confusing. I felt a sense of comfort being back with my mom and missed Vicki and Lee terribly. Wanda told me that Johnny was home from prison and how excited she was to get him back. She told me we had a new place to live and that Vicki and I even had our own room to share. "In two days from now you'll be starting Sycamore Elementary School, Jade, and I already have you and Vicki signed up." My mom seemed proud of herself when she informed me we were not going back to a motel and that I wasn't going to be enrolled late in school that year.

Nick Mills was never mentioned, which was my great fear. She told me she had new clothes and shoes waiting for me. I slept most of the drive home with one eye open. I never felt completely safe when my mom drove, so my sleep was often light. Sometimes I was able to sleep under extreme exhaustion, but it was intermittent unless I had endured a terrible beating or a few nights of lost sleep. There were too many cases in which Wanda had spiraled off the highway or jumped over curbs for me to feel safe when she was in the driver's seat.

Once on the way to Reno, Nevada, we got a flat tire in the snow during the late night hours. Wanda didn't seem to worry about driving alone on snowy highways with bald tires and young children. What confused me was why? Why were we even going to the state of Nevada in the middle of the night? She would yell about the bald tires as we slid about on the highway, but she just kept driving. On this trip, I was her road dog. Sitting in the passenger seat allowed me a front row showing of us slipping across the yellow stripe on one side of the road and almost hitting the guardrails on the other. I contemplated if the guardrails would prevent us from going off the side of the road down the canyon.

Cliffs were another fear of mine, coming so close to the edge of them so often created a paralyzing terror inside me. And it wasn't just with Wanda. Both my parents were scary drivers, mostly because they were under the influence. My dad thought it was comical to speed toward cliffs, hit the dirt, and watch me scream for dear life as the car skated toward the cliff. That, and driving me into dark train tunnels, turning off the lights, and parking while sharing with me that a train could come at any time seemed to amuse him to no end. Watching me scream or sitting frozen in fear sparked hysterics inside of him, causing him to laugh hysterically at my every squeal, terrified expression, scream, and plead for life.

Wanda, on the other hand, was just determined not to let anything stop her from where she wanted to go, even if it meant sleeping in the back of her Volvo with her three kids on the side of a dark highway in the snow. Wanda also had a pattern of forgetting to put the safety on when she was "packing," which was most of the time during those years. I never actually saw her shoot anything intentionally. It was only her accidentals I experienced. Like the time we got a flat on the way to Reno. Wanda laid down the backseats and made a bed which we all climbed into. I was cold and scared as diesels and cars sped by on the dark snowy road.

Wanda had made her way off the road just enough to be tucked in between a couple of Digger Pines but not far enough away that we didn't see the flash of lights coming from every passing vehicle. She pulled out her .357 magnum and reminded us not to touch it right before I felt a vibration shoot throughout my body accompanied by a high pitch ring in my ears. In the distance of the penetrating ring, I could hear Wanda screaming. It took a few seconds for me to realize her gun had gone off, and a bullet had bounced around the four of us before blazing out the side of the Volvo. Which led to Wanda carrying on for hours — superseding the nearly detrimental event.

"Jade, we're here, wake up." As I was awakened by Wanda's voice, I saw in front of me a blue and white stucco house. It had a lawn, and it looked like a fenced backyard. The front door was large and had a fancy golden doorknob. "Is this our house?" I asked. "Sure, is Jadey Pooh." Jadey Pooh was an affectionate term Wanda used when she was happy or happily high. I sheepishly followed her inside our new home, walking straight into Johnny, my stepdad.

Johnny looked bigger than when I had last seen him during one of our conjugal visits at the prison. "Hey, kid," he said as he scooped me up and threw me over his shoulder like I was a ragdoll. I loved Johnny. Looking back later, I could see he was only a big kid caught up with the wrong crowd. I realized his continued growth in size was because he was only 18 years old when my 36-year-old mom seduced him and stole him away from my beautiful older sister. The house was quiet and felt calm. I felt relieved. Johnny lowered me down and told me to go check out my room. I felt a burst of excitement rise inside my belly and started running throughout the house. There were two bathrooms and a large kitchen with beautiful wooden cabinets and marble countertops. Joyfully running, I rushed into my new bedroom.

At first. I stood in the doorway gazing in wonder at what I saw. I wondered if it was really my room or if I had come across a fairy tale. There were two twin-size canopy beds with floral ruffled tops and four curvy white posts. The bedspreads matched the canopy fabric, and white nightstands sat next to each bed.

"Well, what do you think?" I heard my mom ask. I ran to one of the beds and jumped on top. "I love it, mom, thank you." I felt loved by her at that moment, mixed with a little bit of disbelief. I wondered if, somewhere inside, she felt bad for what she and Nick Mills did to me. I wondered if she secretly knew that I had bought her a special gift that she had unknowingly rejected and if she knew how I had sat on the lower step of that motel and cried to myself.

It didn't matter, I told myself as I looked over to see two tall white and gold dressers. I jumped up and ran to the one closest to my bed. I pulled open the drawers to find them stuffed with clothes. "Woo hoo!" I was in heaven. I wondered if this was a new beginning, a new beginning to something wonderful. Maybe this time we would get to stay here. Maybe Johnny wouldn't leave this time. Perhaps the white powder was gone. Wanda did look beautiful and was nice. Everything looked amazing, and there was calm in the atmosphere. I heard Johnny playing his guitar in the living room before I heard him start to sing.

I plopped down in front of him on the carpet. We had carpet! He looked at me while he sang, "*Welcome to the Hotel California. Such a lovely place (such a lovely place). Such a lovely face.*" I felt special, and I felt like he was singing to me. Johnny was so strong and quiet. Somehow his solace transferred into his music. Johnny was even calm right before he fought. He wasn't like the other guys I was used to. Most of the men in my life were loud and bragged about how awesome they were. No, not Johnny. He just seemed to know his strength, and maybe he even doubted it a little, but when the time would come to face off, Johnny would tilt his head up with chin out and wait for the other person to make the first blow, then still in silence I would watch my stepfather beat the person into the ground until they too were silent.

Johnny wasn't untethered like Wanda, although he had been to prison, unlike Wanda. I remember my first visit to San Quentin State prison. It was a visit to the wedding. My mom would marry my sister's high school sweetheart right in front of one of San Quentin's famous murals, and I would be standing right next to her. Next to me was my older sister Diana. She was the eldest of us all and more of a friend to our mom than a daughter. My mom was only 15 years old when she gave birth to Diana, yet married to her first husband already. She first wed when she was 14 years old and would often brag about how she had been a virgin.

Next to Johnny stood his "brothers" Huff and Joker. I knew Huff and Joker as uncles. They would show up on their loud choppers, and they were always together — in and outside of prison, like two black vultures in an everlasting courtship. My mom wore a white dress to wed husband number five, and Johnny wore his flared Levi's, a white "wife-beaters," and his blue bandana, which almost covered his top eyelid. My mom said they got married so we could visit Johnny at the prison because he had earned a new status. By "visit," she meant to stay the weekend.

She also meant she would have the opportunity to sneak drugs and alcohol into the prison for her "old man." I remember the first time Wanda made me her ally. It started before we even left for San Quentin with a six-pack of coke, some syringes, and a bottle of Jack Daniels.

Wanda instructed me carefully to hold the pull tab on top of the coke, lifting it up and turning it to the side just enough to allow the syringe entry. She would draw a few syringes full of coke, releasing them into a bowl sitting next to her. Then load up Jack and shoot a loaded syringe right back into the hole before sealing it with a dap of super glue. Afterward, I would gently let go of the tab allowing it to fall back into place. One of the most important steps in that process was getting the syringe needle as far back as possible underneath the tab to hide and seal the small hole.

Later, we would take Vicki or Lee's baby diapers, depending on who was wearing them at the time, and sow and stitch white powered baggies inside, opening them near the outer seam. My mom would buy pillow stuffing from the fabric store, flatten it, and insert a doubled baggy full of white powder, lacing a couple of pieces of thread throughout the outer bag and connecting it to the newly inserted stuffing. Wanda was an excellent seamstress. She even made my sister Diana's wedding dress prior to her introduction to the white powder. It was a skill she learned growing up so that she could make nice clothes for herself. She was so good at creating beautiful garments that she was hired by a junior college and designed all the costumes for the drama department during my preschool years. But I had not seen her sew anything except patches on jackets and jeans and drugs inside diapers for years. In fact, Wanda sowed a Rolling Stones patch depicting a large red tongue on top of the American flag right over her button flap on her favorite pair of jeans — facing down towards her crotch. I hated that patch. It was so embarrassing. I felt like all eyes were on her female fly when we were in public. I wanted to hide from her but could only distance myself enough to hope I appeared to be someone else's kid.

I was glad Johnny was home and felt like something had changed. I was also excited we wouldn't have to visit the prison anymore. It wasn't so bad being there, I would swing at the playground and play with my siblings. We had our own room inside a nice trailer, but getting into the prison was a nightmare. I knew what my mom was doing was wrong, and her paranoia was worse than her angry outbursts. I, too, felt paranoid. I knew we were taking drugs and alcohol into the prison. When the pack of diapers and six-packs of coke landed on the detectable conveyor belt, my body continued to move, but my soul felt paralyzed. Also, at night Wanda would make her activities with Johnny well-known throughout the trailer. She never kept sex a secret with him or selected others. She had a habit of screaming like she was being murdered while having sex. It was a blood-curdling scream. I didn't dare interrupt her and Johnny. If someone had indeed stabbed her, I would not have known the difference, which was also a fear of mine. I wondered why she screamed like she was being hurt. Especially since sex was not new to me. In fact, I couldn't recall a time in which I didn't know what it was. It simply was. It had always been.

I jumped up when Johnny finished playing his guitar and ran back into my new room. Grandma Georgia passed through my mind. I wished she could see my new room. I imagined her blue eyes sparkling with immense joy as she looked at my new canopy bed with pure delight. I missed her, but I liked our new house, and I was happy Johnny had returned. Even though sometimes things could be scary, even when he was home.

The young sparrow found a nest inside her new house, right there underneath her canopy. She felt air flow through her body and sang her little bird song softly.

Chapter Five
Annie

My first day at Sycamore Elementary School was bittersweet. I walked through the entryway alone, not a single student knowing my name. I had been here before — not at Sycamore Elementary, but alone at a new school. The previous year I had gone to three different schools. The year before that, I went to even more, some schools in different towns and others in different states.

Wanda couldn't remain settled in one spot. Even when things were going well, and there wasn't a reason to move — Wanda would find one. Later, I would ask her why she always wanted to move, even when we didn't have a place of our own to go to. She would respond, "After staying in one place for too long, I felt like the walls were closing in on me." I could relate to that feeling with every new school I started; however, instead of walls closing in on me, eyes from all directions chose me.

"Hi, my name is Mr. Cherry, and I will be your fourth-grade teacher," announced my new wild-haired instructor as he slightly rested on his desk. I immediately liked something about him. He had long, whimsical strawberry blond hair, alert eyes, and an uneven smile, which would leave one corner of his mouth narrow while raising the other — aligning it perfectly with his lifted brow. He had red cheeks the color of immature cherries just before they matured and radiated a spirit of joy from a distance.

I sat at my desk in the room's far back corner. Mr. Cherry let us pick our desks, and while some peers raced to the front, I stayed as far away as possible. I wanted to reduce the number of eyes allowed to look at me. I wanted to be seen but wanted to remain anonymous at the same time. Directly across from me in the middle row sat Annabelle Wright, who sweetly corrected Mr. Cherry when he called out her name.

"I go by Annie," she said as she glanced quickly at me before looking down. Annie had big, beautiful black eyes like polished obsidian. Her skin was black, perfect, and looked smooth. From our first glance, I felt connected to Annie, and I also felt that if I kept our gaze for too long, she would see.

She would see inside of me, inside my innermost hated secrets. The secret was that my Stepdad and his band of brothers were racist. The secret is that my mom had lightning bolts and swastika symbols tattooed on her arm. I was warned that if I ever grew up to have a black boyfriend, my legs and arms would be cut off, and I would be placed by the stubs of my knees on- top of a chain-link fence. I was exposed when Annie's lovely eyes looked into mine — my heart felt an ache and released a thousand silent cries.

Annie's dad was a pilot and flew all over the world. Annie had also been to faraway places like London and Paris. Annie's mom was a nurse like Grandma Drucilla. Her dad's name was Marc, and her mom's name was Cynthia, "Cindy" for short. Cindy always greeted me with a big hug. She had a round face with chubby cheeks and a big smile. She cooked some food I had never eaten before. Her cooking was a party in my mouth and her singing was a gift to my heart. She was always pleased, unlike Wanda. It was as if she liked to be with Annie and me, we were not a burden but "a blessing," she would say. Cindy found ways to encourage me, and she'd shout things from the other room, like, "Girl, you can't sing, but I loveee it when you do..." while chuckling joyfully. "You just keep it up, Jadey girl, don't let anyone tell you to stop singing, you keep using your voice, and one day your voice will use you to bless others."

Cindy gave me a warm place to fall in love with something new that season. She had a warm personal space, which made me feel accepted when I stepped into it. I loved going to Annie's house, even though I wore inside me the consciousness that if Wanda found out where I was going, I would lose Annie forever. I also knew I could never bring Annie to my house, to Vicki, or to Lee. Annie was another secret. And although my adrenaline pumped from school to her house and from her house home, she was a secret worth keeping.

Annie's house wasn't too far from mine, so I could walk to and from. Wanda wasn't worried about meeting my friends' parents, perhaps because they were in constant rotation because we were always on the move. She rarely asked me for an address or phone number. Still, my walks home from Annie's house included me looking over my shoulder like I was being watched and had done something wrong. I wanted to tell Annie and her mother about my real life, but I couldn't. How could I hurt this loving family by telling them about the hate that filled mine? My blanket of shame would cover me as I walked home, but the Helper inside of my spirit would whisper — "Hating people because their skin color is different than yours is evil, and you, Jade, are not evil. You are not like the Peckerwoods or Wanda, you are different. Never stop being you."

The Sparrow feared too much white in her environment. It was the white that harmed her. The white powder and the proud white peckerwoods. The Sparrow knew deep inside her heart it wasn't really about colors, but about good versus evil. The Sparrow and a beautiful Starling found true friendship in each other against the Sparrow's adversities.

Chapter Six
Unfortunate One

A few months had passed since I had started attending Sycamore Elementary School. Things were beginning to look a lot like middle class madness inside our blue house. I knew we weren't the typical middle-class folks like Annie and her family, but we were living among them. Madness had seeped back into our beautiful new space. Huff and Joker were released from prison and were our part-time house guests. Nights were again filled with blazing music, pot, and now what I called meth instead of white powder. Peckerwoods were in and out all hours of the night, making sleep challenging. I knew no one in my house cared about my report cards or my homework, but I wanted to turn in my homework for Mr. Cherry, he seemed to care. But most times, it was hard to focus because it was loud and there were so many people, and sometimes Johnny's band of brothers walked around our living room and said things my ears seemed to gravitate towards.

"Johnny, check this out," Joker said with excitement as they threw an army bag on the floor along with several other items I didn't recognize. "Idiot thought I needed a ride. He went for one, that's for sure..." chuckling. Joker was tall and skinny with long stringy blonde hair. He always wore black leather like Huff. He looked like Tigger from Winnie the Pooh when he talked because he bounced with each word.

Huff had long dark hair and wore an even longer biker mustache. I watched as Joker poured the army bag's contents onto the coffee table, some spilling over onto the floor. He and Huff were so excited. Johnny looked up and tilted his head with approval. Joker laughed. "Punk's on the bottom of the canyon now," as he continued to pillage through this man's belongings. I soon realized the man who had owned this green army bag and the backpack was most likely dead. Huff continued to share how he and Joker plotted a hitch-hike hoist. Some nice guy was on his way to a private hike to get some comfort and made the serious mistake of picking these two up.

"Fool told us everything, blah blah blah blah," Joker continued as he made an inappropriate hand gesture that involved his privates. "Asked him to pull over so I could take a leak before I slammed fool boys head into the steering wheel." "Get anything else, or did you off this guy for an army sack full of clothes and a backpack? Aunt Marla laughed. Aunt Marla was Johnny's baby sister. She was the youngest of five boys. All five being a "Peckerwood" and Aunt Marla being a "Featherwood." A Featherwood was the female equivalent of the male Peckerwood. Both belonged to the same racist prison gang. Wanda was proud of herself when she earned the title of "Featherwood."

I continued to imagine this innocent guy's face being slammed into his steering wheel from behind before Joker strangled him. When he realized that his kind gesture had just turned, I imagined his shock. I pictured Joker and Huff's amusement as they threw this innocent man's body over the hill and down into the steep crevice. *Was he young or was he old? Did he have a family that loved him*? I wondered. My heart felt sore as I saw this scene play out in my mind. They were so happy to take this guy's life. I felt like I was going to throw up, but I didn't dare show any discomfort. I was just a little girl, hidden by their oblivion. Yet, I was no longer innocent or naive. I understood what happened. I knew it was wrong. I also understood I had cause to fear for my life. I knew if I said anything to anyone, I, too, would be at the bottom of a gorge somewhere or worse. These guys were a different breed from Nick Mills, a different kind of evil.

Strangely, they boasted about the way they protected me. No, the Peckerwoods never physically hurt me, nor did they ever touch me like the other men Wanda brought around or left me with when Johnny was in prison. They talked about how they killed child molesters and prided themselves on it. They somehow missed the fact that snorting drugs while telling me not to do it, having sex with my mom or sisters where I could see or overhear, celebrating murdering people in front of me, having me hold guns, weigh drugs, hide them on my body, and telling me how they would lose all love for me if I ever had a black friend was NOT protecting me. No, all of that was okay, it was what fueled their existence. It was also my life, oddly enough, and although I wanted it to be different, I, too, was fueled with excitement when new clothes were delivered to me in exchange for meth or pot.

I saw a glimpse of myself as I watched Joker cheerfully bounce around the living room while he pulled dollar bills out of the unsuspecting hiker's black wallet. I imagined pulling clothes out of a black garbage bag with joy, knowing they were stolen, tags still on. It beat wearing clothes from a thrift store, which had often been the case. I didn't want to be like Joker, and I didn't want my things to be stolen. I was relieved to have new clothes, but they came with a cost — each item added another layer to my shame. Another secret to tuck deep into my soul, another lie to hide, and another cover that I would have to create.

I looked over at the clock and saw it was 11:40 pm. Shoot. I thought. I have to get up for school at 6:30 a.m. I decided to leave the tall tales of Joker and Huff to the living room group and head to bed. When I went to bed, I felt the normal knots in my stomach, only this time, I felt more pain than the hurt associated with affliction. As I laid there, the pain grew. I fluffed my pillow and pushed it into my stomach under me, but it did little to reduce the growing throb in my abdomen. I could hear people leaving and thought of calling for my mom, but she hated it when I disturbed her during the night. She hated it when I complained of being sick, especially if it involved a trip to the doctor or dentist. How could a woman who was so brazen when it came to sneaking drugs into a prison be so intimidated by a doctor, I often wondered.

My face began to feel like it was on fire, it hurt, and the pain was getting worse. I looked at my alarm clock, and it was now 2:00 am. I couldn't sleep. I felt like I was being stabbed in my gut. The throbbing wouldn't stop no matter what I did. Finally, around 5:00 am, I dozed off just before my alarm clock went off. I slept for an hour and a half; it wasn't enough. I was accustomed to going to school tired, but I felt sick. I felt a lump in my throat, afraid to say anything to Wanda, I stumbled to my dresser. I started opening a drawer, but I felt weak. I was dizzy and nauseous. I couldn't do it. I looked over at Vicki, still sleeping peacefully, and decided to pretend my alarm clock didn't go off, which added to my stomachache. It felt so good to crawl back into bed underneath the covers. The intense throbbing that plagued me throughout the night had subsided — I fell fast asleep.

"Jade, what the hell...why are you sleeping? Get up, get up right now," screamed Wanda. I was jarred awake as I saw Wanda pull Vicki out of her bed. "You're gonna get CPS called on me, you little bitch" she kept shouting. "Dammit Jade, I can't trust you to do anything." Wanda had a strong fear of social services. It was like she thought they had a personal mission to come after her, just as my father feared the government. "Mom, I'm sick, my stomach hurts, and I was up all night," I replied. "Ya, right, and I can magically fly to the moon and back. Get up, Jade, don't expect me to fall for your bullshit." "But I'm sick. My stomach hurts really bad," I said as tears flowed from my eyes. "I don't want to go," I started to shout. "I do not want to get dressed!" I didn't want to go to school to see Mr. Cherry or Annie like this. I could only imagine what I looked like, and worse was the idea of making it throughout the day.

"Get your damn clothes on now" my mom's eyes turned black — lost was her jadeite sparkle. I cried, "No. I can't. I won't." Wanda screamed as she grabbed my hair and swung me around, throwing me onto the floor. I grabbed the top of my head as I watched her walk towards me. Her hand reached down and grabbed a batch of my hair that she used to pull me to my feet. Her arms pushed me toward my dresser before I felt a kick to my back, plummeting me into my white dresser with the gold handles. "Okay, okay, I'll get dressed," I said through my tears.

Wanda was madder than a wet hen, as my Grandma, Georgia, would have said as she dropped Vicki and me off in front of our school. Before we were sent to our classrooms. I walked into the office with my sister and a scribbled note in my hand. I tried to hide my embarrassment as I walked my late slip up to Mr. Cherry. I wanted to disappear. There was nowhere to hide, nowhere to go. I wanted to die. When I got back to my desk, I saw that Annie wasn't at hers. It would be even worse now, I thought, but at the same time, I wouldn't have to hide what had happened. I knew Annie would be able to tell something had happened to me or at least see how awful I felt.

That night things only got worse. I ran to the bathroom and made it there just in time to throw up inside the toilet. Another severe wave of nausea would hit me before I could leave the bathroom. I put my face on the bathroom floor. The cool tile felt good against my burning cheeks. My stomach pained me so badly that I had to muffle my moans with each stabbing sensation. Once again, the pain subsided in the early hours of the morning, just before it was time to get dressed for school.

This would repeat itself that entire week until one day, Annie told Mr. Cherry I was sick, but I was afraid to go to the office. I had finally told Annie what was going on after her prompting, and my sweet friend didn't have the capability to hold secrets like me. Mr. Cherry asked me to stay during recess and took me to the office after a few questions. This led to the school nurse repeatedly trying to contact my mom, which was a no-go because the number they had was not a working number. Soon I heard the nurse talk to my principal.

My breathing was shallow and fast when I thought of Wanda, but I was too weak to fight. Too weak to do anything. I just rested on the bed in the nurse's office. I wondered if I could just stay there and sleep until I got better. My eyes were closed when I felt a tap on my shoulder. I looked up to see Mr. Williams, my principal. He was short with brown eyes and hair. He helped me sit up as he softly shared with me that he was going to give me a ride home. Even in 1984, that was a rare practice, but I didn't fight it. I was glad I was going home. I was glad he was taking me. Embarrassment would peak its ugly head, but I was too sick to let it overtake me.

Mr. Williams had a red sports car and put me right in the front seat, where I rested my head against the passenger door. He stopped at our blue house, immediately came to me, opened the door, and helped me out of the car. He was so gentle. I had never experienced his kind of chivalry. He walked slowly next to me, approaching the front door. He knocked, no answer. Looking down at me, he said, "I'm going to do my best to find your mom, okay?" He bent his head against the door as he knocked harder. I knew he could hear the music I heard. He knocked even harder, his gentle demeanor changing slightly. The door opened, and there stood Wanda in her white silk slip.

"Are you Wanda Spencer?" Wanda looked surprised and stood in the doorway, speechless. "Are you Wanda Spencer?" Mr. Williams asked again abruptly. "Ya, what's going on?" She replied. I put my head down. I didn't want to see anymore. It was terrible. My principal saw my mom in her sleazy slip. I wanted to crawl into a hole and die alone somewhere. "Look at your daughter Ma'am. Do you not see how yellow she is? Look at her eyes and her skin! Your daughter is very sick. Have you not noticed her swollen liver bulging out of her belly? You get this kid to the doctor right away, or I'm calling CPS. And one more thing," yelled Mr. Williams as he walked away, "if you ever send that child to school like that again, you will have me to answer too."

Wanda begrudgingly did exactly what Mr. Williams instructed her to do and learned I had contracted Hepatitis A. Vicki and Lee had to get shots so they wouldn't catch it from me. So, did anyone else who cared about their health. I was allowed to stay home and rest now that Wanda didn't have to worry about having the CPS called on her or her getting cut off welfare. I was so grateful for Mr. Williams. He didn't even know me, but he fought for me and stood up to Wanda. I thanked the Helper for Annie, the school nurse, and Mr. Williams. For days I laid in my canopy bed in agony as my small body recovered. The house calmed down with the knowledge that Hepatitis was in the house. Johnny asked people to stay away and told them he was going to go to them. Johnny occasionally brought me home a kid's meal and would sit on my bed with me. He'd say, "You'll be better soon, kid."

The sparrow rested as her belly healed from the arrow puncture. The arrow had pierced her side, inflicting terrible pain, but before the arrow made its way to her lower abdomen, it penetrated her heart as thoughts about the unfortunate one passed through her mind. How she wished she could spread her wings and find the deep canyon in which his lifeless body lay.

Chapter Seven
Guns and Gorillas

Cindy opened the door, "Well, hello, Jadey girl, it's good to see you." Annie's mom embraced me. Behind her, I could see a beautiful, tall Christmas tree, the pine aroma filled the air. It reminded me of the time I went up into the mountains with my dad and walked through the forest. The tree was beautifully decorated. It sparkled like shiny diamonds from top to bottom. We didn't have a Christmas tree inside our blue house. Wanda was allergic to pine trees and did not believe in Christmas. She sometimes bought me, Vicki, and Lee a gift around that time, depending on where we were, but they weren't wrapped and perfectly placed underneath a tree like at Annie's house.

"How've you been, my sweet girl?" Cindy asked. I joyfully replied, "Good!" Really, I had been recovering from a black eye and fat lip after Wanda had one of her rages. Cindy and Annie seemed to have a special gift for sniffing things out when it came to me. I learned to hide from them as much as possible when I was hurt because I knew they would zoom in on my wounds. I felt like I was always hiding something. Hiding my best friend, Annie, so the Peckerwoods wouldn't off me or hurt Annie's family. Hiding my life from Cindy and Annie. Hiding my wounds from the world around me...

I was happy for Annie. I loved that she had a good mom and dad. She had bedtime and chores, and her parents didn't call her bad names, pull her hair or pummel her in the head until she bled. While on the floor, Annie had never been kicked by her mother or told how she was a "hateful, mean, ugly little bitch." I never understood why Wanda would scream those words repeatedly as she beat me. Was I mean and hateful? I didn't try to be. I tried to be good. I even tried to help Wanda. I got up for school and helped Vicki get ready for school as well. Wanda consistently told me I was like my dad. "Mean, hateful, and crazy," as she would beat me until I had no more screams left inside me. Her blows wouldn't end until my yells stopped and turned into soft whimpers because I was too weak to scream or cry for help. I'd often be left on the floor, my cheek pressed into the shaggy carpet, the taste of blood filling my mouth, my face heating up like it was a wood stove rising in temperature, and the sound of my head beating inside my ears. She would always end by asking, "Are you happy now?" No, I wasn't happy. I was hurt. Physically my body was injured, but more than the pain that penetrated my cells was the arrow that pierced my heart. I felt like a piece of trash Wanda was forced to carry around. Sometimes, I wished I would die during one of those blows, so she could throw me out with the rest of the garbage.

Things had become a Peckerwood jungle again at home. People flooded in and out all hours of the night. The chaos would slow down around 4 in the morning. That's usually when I got the best sleep until my alarm clock went off. It had been four months, and I hadn't seen my dad or gone to the grandparents' house. My life was anchored to the blue grand central station in a blue-collar neighborhood. By this time, neighbors had become concerned and filed complaints due to traffic and noise. When I would leave for school in the mornings, I would see older neighbors staring at me. The eyes had diminished at school but grew around outside of the blue house.

Johnny was gone a lot during this time, and Wanda was already sharing her bed with other men. One day, I heard her telling my older sisters she had fulfilled her Featherwood duties. Mainly speaking, having sex with Peckerwoods who were recently released from prison. Drug drops were usually part of the exchange. Meth was constantly weighed and packed right in our living room. We had our very own assembly line of white powder and on duty Peckerwoods.

A late-night exchange had just taken place, and people had been commissioned to make their deliveries. When I heard my belly grumble, I realized how hungry I was. Wanda was busy stashing the rest of the drug booty into a secret space Johnny had made. I jumped up on the cool marble kitchen counter, laughed and made gorilla sounds in hopes of getting Vicki and Lee to join me. They thought it was funny when I made gorilla gestures accompanied by noises. I opened a cabinet door that hung over the refrigerator in search of some cereal. Opening it and closing it, making gorilla noises, "OOh OOh..." when I heard the door on the other side of the frig bust open.

Before I could move, two people stood next to me, facing me in full-faced ski masks while holding machine guns. Eyes wide open and frozen, I looked at them, then at Vicki and Lee. One of the big men motioned with his gun for me to get down. He didn't say a word as he lifted his index finger to his mouth. I knew what he was telling me to do. He was saying, get down, don't say a word, and go to your brother and sister. I felt my heartbeat beating inside my throat. This wasn't the first time I had a gun pointed at me, but something inside me told me these guys weren't playing around. Not that the others had been. I began to operate like a robot, my mind processed the input it was receiving, and my body quickly responded to all commands.

I jumped down and went to Vicki and Lee. I quickly complied with what I believed I was silently being told to do. I whispered to Vicki and Lee, "Shoo, we are playing cops and robbers..." I opened a lower cabinet door and said, "Come here, let's hide," as I heard Wanda yell, "What's going on out there?" The stillness inside me swiftly shifted into panic once again. Would this be it? Is this how I was going to die? Would they let Vicki and Lee live? I would do anything they wanted if they left my little brother and sister alone.

God, if you can hear me, please save Vicki and Lee, I began to pray inside my head. I heard Wanda coming as the two robbers braced themselves in front of me. Wanda came around the kitchen corner and came to a dead stop. She screamed one of her blood-curdling screams when she saw what stood over me. My mom seemed so small and terrified at that moment. She didn't seem so powerful and dark, but like a little blonde rag doll as one of the robbers hit her upside her head with his gun. She dropped to the floor. Blood drained from her head. "Kid get me a pillow," yelled one of the men with a deep raspy voice. I ran into my room and grabbed my pillow, ran back, and handed it to him. I didn't want him to kill my mom, but maybe if I did what they asked, they would let Vicki and Lee live. Vicki and Lee were innocent.

Wanda yelled out, "You dirty Bastards! You're gonna get it when Johnny hears..." before she could say another word, the pillow was over her head with a gun pointed at her back. "Shut the fuck up, say another word, and your dead woman, and so are your brats," fired back one of the thieves as he slammed his gun into her back.

"Where are the drugs?" Shouted the other. "Where are they?" "I don't have any here," Wanda replied. "Bullshit, you really want to die tonight, don't you? But first, you're gonna get to watch your kids die." The other guy walked over to me, I looked him in his eyes, but his gaze only told me there was no wiggle room, no amount of charm I could muster up would change his end goal. He had a dead gaze which revealed this would not be his first murder. Vicki and Lee were yelling at this point.

The man who stood over me, Vicki and Lee, grabbed my hair and told me to "shut it up" while the other robber pulled Wanda's hair, revealing her blood covered face and newly missing front tooth. Her hair spoiled in blood, she looked at us and then looked me dead in the eyes. I was silent and felt like I had been submerged under water, unable to breathe since they had kicked in the door. Vicki and Lee screamed at the top of their lungs when I was pulled up by my hair and when they saw our mom's bloody face. They knew we weren't playing cops and robbers anymore, nor were we in the jungle with a troop of gorillas — there was nothing I could do to calm them. "Mom, tell them... tell them, please, mom tell them..." I pleaded. "Shut the hell up, Jade." "You're a Stupid Bitch" shouted the robber, who hit her again with his gun, busting another seam that held her face together.

"I know where they are," I yelled. "Please stop." It hurt me to see Wanda being beaten and bloodied. I loved her even though she didn't like me. I loved her and wished I was strong enough to protect her, but I couldn't fight these men with their guns. *Why wasn't Johnny or the peckerwoods here when we needed them?* I wondered.

"Get up," yelled the man standing over her. Wanda got up and used her hand to pull her bloody hair away from her face as she thrust her head back like a tough thug, although it was vividly apparent she was helpless. The only power she possessed now was the withholding of her drugs and money.

"Mom, please tell them," I shouted, realizing the man had tightened his grip on my hair. "Fine, you Bastards." The man's grip on my hair loosened. "I'll stay here, you go," he shouted. I sat down and wrapped my arms around Vicki and Lee. "It's gonna be okay, it's gonna be okay," I told them as they buried their little bodies into mine. The man with my mom returned to gather us up, and with the two guns pointed to our backs, we walked to Wanda and Johnny's bedroom.

There in the corner below their king-size waterbed, we huddled together. I closed my eyes and silently prayed again, *Please God save Vicki and Lee, please, they didn't do anything. I'm bad, ugly, hateful. Wanda's bad, but they are good. Please let them live.* Just then I heard one of the men say, "Start counting backward from 100, NOW!" he screamed... I opened my eyes inside the dark room as I heard my mom start to count. As she counted 100, 99, 98, I saw the two big bodies fade into the darkness. I could hear them throwing things around and rustling through things. At one point, I heard the man with the deeper voice scream "Count Louder" from the other room. My mom increased her volume so they could hear her. I was relieved Wanda was complying and wasn't trying to find her gun. I could feel her anger, I could hear her anger with every number she said, but my mom stayed there by us.

Thank you, God, I kept saying inside my mind. *Thank you. You're true, and you love Vicki and Lee as I do. You know they are good, and you saved them.* I knew the men weren't gone and could come back and shoot us at any minute, but I had to believe what my grandparents had taught me. I had no one else at that moment. I didn't fully trust that Wanda would continue to put us before her drugs and money. She could decide to stop counting at any moment.

But God was bigger than anything, even guns, my grandparents said. Grandma Georgia had told me to pray to him when I needed help, and he would send the Helper. She told me the Helper wouldn't always help me the way I wanted to be helped, but to trust He would help me. She told me to listen carefully and to be still and to thank God for sending His Helper. I knew the Helper loved me. I just wondered why he couldn't make all the bad go away. Why couldn't He make Wanda like Cindy and Gary like Marc? But at this moment — I knew the Helper had given me the strength to stay calm, the strength not to cry, and the strength to encourage Wanda to surrender.

The sparrow nestling covered her sibling hatchlings in the corner of that dark room underneath the wooden ledge of the waterbed's frame and waited for the strangers' footsteps to walk out the front door.

Chapter Eight
Uncle Pete

As soon as Wanda heard tires peel out in the driveway and the sound of a muffler fade into the distance, she was up and running to see what had been taken. I sat for a moment longer with Vicki and Lee waiting in the darkness. I was still afraid and didn't know if the men would come back, but I finally mustered up the courage to help Wanda. Vicky and Lee tagged along behind me. My mom frantically searched through the space Johnny had carved out in the wall. A space that had been covered by a framed poster of Hitler.

When Wanda saw that all the drugs and money were gone, she began to pound her fist against the wall and scream bloody murder. I stood there watching her. She looked like a character from a splatter film. Her blonde hair was covered with dry, dark blood making it difficult to see her golden locks. Her right front tooth was missing, her lips swollen, and her eyes blackening.

She pounded the wall screaming louder and louder until she picked up a lamp that was set on an end table and threw it across the room. Then she flipped the coffee table over — kicking it repeatedly. Vicki and Lee looked up at me like two startled owls, eyes wide, and confused. They were both so timid and tiny.

Wanda turned her attention towards me, walking over, she shouted, "Jade, you were gonna narc me out, you little

Narc!" I looked up at her as she stood hovering over me like a demon with skin on. The robbers had left, but the devil still stood in the living room. I had a sinking feeling inside my stomach. She would get even. I knew her pattern. I could see it, and before I had even finished the thought, Wanda commanded me to fill me and Vicki's pillowcases with clothes.

I made haste to do as she commanded. I came out of the bedroom, pillowcases in my hands, and sprinted to the kitchen, where I could hear water running and Wanda's voice. Her head dipped underneath the faucet. The water turned dark blood bright red once again. She wrapped her hair and grabbed the landline, and started desperately trying to get a hold of Johnny, but the calls ended quickly. No one knew where Johnny was.

She told me to get into the car with Vicky and Lee as I watched her running around the house like one of the chickens my dad cut the head off of. It dawned on me that my mom, who had prided herself so much on her beauty, who competed with her oldest daughters, who didn't allow her grandchildren to use the term "grandma" in her presence, was now running throughout the house, and didn't even seem to notice she had a missing tooth.

We packed into the white Volvo about 20 minutes after the robbers fled away. Wanda drove like a wild woman down backstreets while thinking someone was after us. Then hit the freeway... a few moments later, she swiftly flew off the interstate, landing in a side ditch.

"Damn it, damn it..." she screeched while slamming both hands on the steering wheel. I was in another horror movie. No one knew, and no one would care. My body ached, a strange pain I didn't understand, but more than that was the numbness I sat with on the inside. Fear had withered into unresponsiveness once again — robbing my adrenaline.

I reverted back into the robot version of me. A robot with a human heart somewhere deep inside playing an emotionless rhythm that echoed loudly inside its tin shell. Wanda was able to get out of the ditch and back onto the freeway. She yelled, "Jade, you're going to your dad's." Why did she always yell? I hated how she always yelled.

Oh well, it didn't matter now. I knew where I was headed. Wanda's screams would be reserved for someone else. I wondered where Vicky and Lee would go. What would happen to them, and how long it would be before I saw them again.

Wanda raced down the windy road past the red barn and made a hard right onto the grandparents' street before quickly parking in front of their house. It was late and dark, but my dad's bedroom light was on. Wanda got out and ran across the lawn. I said my goodbyes to Vicki and Lee and told them everything was going to be okay. That they were going somewhere safe and that I would see them again soon.

I felt guilty then for lying to them, but I needed to see them leave with some solace.

I stood holding my pillowcase full of what would be my belongings for the next several months as Wanda ran over to my dad's window, "Gary, Gary" she shouted. The light was on. So, I thought he was awake, but the rest of the house was dark. His thick tie-dye blanket, which covered his window, pulled to the side, and someone with long dark hair peeked out. I could see she was young and pretty from a distance. Dad must have a new girlfriend, I thought.

The front door opened; my dad stood there in his boxers. "What's going on, Wanda?" he asked. "I was robbed, Gary. I was robbed of everything and held at gunpoint." My dad flipped the porch light on and looked at her, and said, "My god, you look awful." To which she replied, "Jade's gonna stay with you for a while." Behind my dad emerged the dark-haired girl. She was beautiful and young. He introduced her as Titania.

Titania had long dark straight hair and big brown sultry eyes. She was tall and thin, reminding me of some of the girls I saw in magazines and in movies. Compared to my mom, she looked like one of my older sisters instead of a potential stepmother. But she looked nice and quickly smiled at me, I returned the smile. I was glad to see my dad had a new girlfriend. He always picked beautiful girlfriends, and even though they did not stay around for long, most were kind to me.

My dad welcomed me inside. The house was silently sleeping. I smelled pot. I knew it was coming from dad's room. Smoking pot was allowed inside my dad's bedroom at the grandparents' house. It seemed to calm my dad, and Grandma would allow anything that made him happy.

Wanda left quickly without so much as a "goodbye Jade" or a hug. Just like a star that falls too fast, they were gone. I walked inside the house, and my dad went and got a blanket and pillow and made a bed for me on the couch, which was my bed at my grandparents' house. My dad looked sober, which was a relief. I felt as though it was a little kiss from heaven that he had a girlfriend and that he wasn't drunk.

Everything was quiet as I lay on the couch and thought about Vicky and Lee. I knew my stays with my dad were short-lived, and I would see them again, but who would play with them and comfort them in my absence? I continued to reflect on the night just enough to say another silent prayer —to tell God that I knew it was Him who helped us and saved us from those men. I asked Him, *please, God, send your Helper to watch over Vicki and Lee and take care of them and please help Wanda God. Please help her be a mom like other mommies. And please, God, help her to see I'm not bad.*

I drifted off into a deep sleep while praying. The next morning, I woke early to the smell of bacon and eggs. I realized how hungry I was. I hadn't eaten since I had a sandwich at lunchtime the day before. The food smelled so good I got up and went into the kitchen. My Grandma was cooking on her green gaslit stove.

She turned around and looked at me with a calm razor-edged smile, and said, "Good morning, Jade." And then quickly turned back. Uncle Pete sat at the table's far end opposite Grandma's back. He was reading the morning newspaper. I went and sat down next to him as he gestured for me to do so. Uncle Pete always looked like a cartoon character to me. I would feel slightly queasy when I saw him simply because he was so creepy. Uncle Pete also had another bad habit beside his snorting tick. He was a pervert!

I sat down next to him at the table, as my Grandma turned her back to cook, he hit me on my knees underneath the table with his newspaper. I was barely awake. I didn't understand. I thought maybe he was just playing a game. I looked at him with a certain amount of irritation and strength. Unlike other men who intimidated me, Uncle Pete didn't frighten me as much. Maybe it was because I had been exposed to his antics since birth, or maybe it was because he was the low man on the totem pole in the grandparents' house.

I knew he was still stronger and bigger than me, and I still wasn't brave enough to tell any of the secrets we shared. But there was something inside me that felt defiant when I looked at him. He also looked like one of those tiny little leprechauns I would see on a cereal box at the end of a rainbow standing next to a pot of gold. But he didn't hold any gold in his hands. Instead, he would hold something nasty. Something I shouldn't have seen and didn't want to see.

Uncle Pete turned his newspaper around to reveal his dirty magazine smoothly lining the inside of the Daily News. Two women were fully engaged and fully exposed. I looked at him with disgust. He was a dirty little weirdo. As he produced a hiccup-slash-snort while his upper body jerked— he showed me the next page. When my grandma turned around, he would lift his newspaper, so she thought he was simply reading the news. Then he would turn the paper back around, rub the woman's private parts, and act like he was pinching their nipples.

Laughing, snorting, and hiccupping while he twitched. I had gotten some sleep, but I still felt so weak from the night before, and I was hungry. I just wanted breakfast. But I had Pete the Perverted Leprechaun sitting next to me. I felt like I couldn't escape. I couldn't escape my life of madness. Grandma brought me over my breakfast, I did my best to ignore him with eyes that screamed leave me alone, or I might tell on you.

My intense glares failed to scare him. As Grandma left the kitchen, he unzipped his pants and pulled out his hairy penis covered in red mangy hair. "Hehehe...," he continued to laugh as he exposed himself to me. He stroked himself wildly like an orangutan in the zoo before smearing a white substance all over the naked ladies in the magazine. My breakfast lost all appeal. My hunger was gone, along with any innocence I had left.

My dad and Titania were still sleeping. Sleep away, daddy, sleep away.

The little sparrow played alone in the backyard. Pressing her beak against the sticker's edge. Spreading her wings, she flew around the lovely grazing cows on the other side of the fence. In an open field behind the grandparents' house, she found moments of freedom.

Chapter Nine
Fire on the Hillside

The rest of Christmas break was filled with Dad and Titania's romance. They met at AA and were entangled like two ballet dancers. She was kind and loved to jump on my dad's lap. My dad just got mad at me once during that visit. Grandma took me to Sears to allow me to pick out my own "big" Christmas present. I chose a pink children's sewing machine instead of a boy's bike.

"Come on, Jade, get the bike," my dad said while running his hand through his dark hair. I was getting stronger on the inside. A little braver because I refused to get the bike and walked out with my dad carrying a little girl's sewing machine. It bothered me that he was upset, but I stuck with my decision and didn't waiver. Dad was sober and had a friend, so I felt a sense of ease to do what I wanted to do. If Dad had been Drunk Gary, the Drunk Gary who pushed me down into the dark crawl space beneath his bedroom before closing the hole with its baseboard cover — I would have gone with the bike.

Uncle Pete continued to reveal himself as often as he could find a quick chance to do so but never got a chance to be alone with me for too long. Dad's sobriety shielded me from his midnight molestations. Grandpa Pay and I played Bingo and searched the yard for special stones while Grandma taught me how to use my new sewing machine.

Things were always awkward at the grandparents' house. I didn't feel like it was my home, and something always felt eerie to me. My soul waited in a state of distress. Waited for Wanda to return. And when that day came…I was ready.

Wanda emerged scattered and tattered. Yet, there she was, standing in the middle of my grandparents' house, shouting about how Johnny left her for a younger woman who had four kids of her own. How Johnny had been with her the night of the robbery and how he told her they had nothing else now that the "last of the load was gone." My grandparents sat on their love-seat like two stuffed animals pushed up against each other, no words. I looked around and realized no one in the living room seemed to care about a word Wanda had to say. Dad was preoccupied with Titania, and Uncle Al and Pete just sat on their chairs, nodding. She hardly looked at me. Why didn't she hug me? Did she feel anything but hate for me? She always came back. Was it just for the welfare check?

I was saying my goodbyes when I overheard her tell my dad that my sister Diana was in the car with her two kids, Vicki and Lee, and that we were leaving the state. It would be another night's drive. Wanda threw me a nightgown and told me to prepare for a night in the back of the Volvo. A bed was already made. Vicki and Lee were in it! I ran to the bathroom and said goodbyes again as Wanda led me out the door. Grandpa Pay always said the best goodbyes, "I'll see you next time," with a nod, a pocket full of change, and a loving smile. I loved him and would miss him. I doubted I would see Titania again, but I made sure to send her a smile of approval before closing the door behind me.

It was a cold, dry winter night, but we were as snug as small bugs in the back of the Volvo. Wanda had laid the seats down and made us a bed. I was happy to be back cuddling with Vicki, Lee, and my two nieces. Wanda started south on I-5... Leaving our town, the blue house in the blue collared neighborhood, Johnny and Annie... The hatchback made into a bed, and the joy-filled reunion with Vicki and Lee somehow seemed to erase the thoughts of what I had lost. Losing wasn't new, gain and loss had been our life. Few things stayed the same with Wanda. We were off again on a new trip down an unknown road to an unknown place, an unknown school, and an unknown town.

I liked the long girly nightgown made from cotton she had brought for me. Wanda didn't get new nightgowns when she was a little girl. Grandma Georgia didn't buy her new clothes when she was young, and from what Wanda said, Georgia would send her to school with a brown paper bag containing one drop biscuit inside. Wanda said the other children laughed at her and told me how humiliated she was. She, too, at one time felt like all the eyes in the classroom chose her just to "make a spectacle out of something."

She would tell me how she didn't get her first new dress until she married Leroy at 14 years old and how later after her good-looking, sexy Italian husband cheated on her with other men, she moved back in with Georgia. How her older sister, "Georgia's favorite," had also lived there with her children during a split from her husband. And because her eldest sister had been shot in the head by their older brother, Georgia gave "Juney all the attention."

How she would work all day in the strawberry fields with a broken heart and bloody fingers from the thorns to a house full of dishes and dirt. While Juney sat around and read the Bible with Georgia. Wanda was told she either did the dishes or her and my sisters could leave, according to Wanda that is. However, there was an obvious disconnect between Wanda and Georgia, and either by brainwashing or awareness, I had observed the favoritism she complained about.

My mom had dropped me off at Grandma Georgia's, but she never stayed there, not as long as I had been alive. No matter the case, she refused to stay at Georgia's. Even when we were sleeping in the car and bathing at the dock.

Wanda and Diana cruised down the freeway listening and singing along to some of their favorite Willie Nelson tunes. "*Bridges over covered waters*" was one of my mom's favorite songs when she was clean. We were approximately 45 minutes into our journey south when I felt a sense of danger arise in my spirit. A feeling I had grown to discern, being more attuned to my surroundings than most of the children I knew. A gift that was recognized early by my dysfunctional childlike parents.

I sat up abruptly as the sensation of danger swelled inside of me. My eyes turned to the dark freeway that moved quickly behind us. As I studied the black asphalt and white road stripes diminishing in the rear windshield — I saw a flash. Another immediately followed. Now my eyes were peeled to the pavement that fell away so swiftly behind us. Suddenly I saw a flame that left sparks dancing down the freeway.

I shouted out, "Mom, there's a fire, the car is on fire!" Turning down Willie in order to hear me better, Wanda responded, "Jade, what are you talking about now?" I proceeded to cry out, detailing how I had first seen sparks and then a flame. She looked out the back via the use of her rear-view mirror and ordered me to stop bothering her. I had acquired a bit of a mischievous sense of humor at times when I didn't feel the threat of death, but this was not a joke.

"There's no fire," replied my mom as she turned the radio back up. She and my eldest sister continued humming along to one of Willie's songs, "*maybe I didn't love you quite as often as I could have.*" It was then that I saw a monstrous-looking flame sweep upwards from the back of the car leaving a golden glow upon the dark road. "Fire, fire!" I screamed. At that point, I was not going to back down. Wanda started to get pissed as she looked out her rear-view mirror and saw no indication of fire, no sparks, no flames.

All she saw and heard was me shrieking in pure horror. Finally, she pulled the Volvo over, parked on the shoulder near a hillside that was covered in dry weeds, and immediately got out to address me. I watched as her body moved towards the back of the car when suddenly she stopped. I dreaded the thought of one of her fierce beatings, but I feared being roasted to death in the car much more. I next saw her body lean forward when she stooped down and then yelled, " Get out of the car, get out...Fire, there's fire!"

Doors flew open, and the next thing I knew, I was racing down the freeway in my long nightgown carrying my pillowcase of clothes. I glanced back just in time to see the car engulfed by flames. The flames wrapped around the Volvo when BAM...! The fire ignited the gas tank producing an explosion that sent me stumbling into a trench. I waited there while my mom, sister, siblings, and nieces shot down the freeway. I watched as fires began to form on the hillside, swiftly growing and spreading.

I laid below the irrigation tunnel filled with cold water up to my knees and watched the fire climb the hillside. How did I know of the danger before I saw it? I set up when I had discerned danger, then saw sparks. My eyes widened while knee deep in the cold ditch water with the awareness of what had just transpired as the fire trucks, cops, and ambulances arrived.

I realized at that moment I could trust myself and only myself. I realized I had a gift others didn't have. Was it the Helper? I didn't know, but from that point on... I knew my gift had saved us.

The Sparrow heard whispers of danger and braved the flames. She, the Sparrow, was confident in the voice now. She realized she possessed a superpower that would help her one day — help her fly far, far away.

Chapter Ten
Awakening

The Volvo folded like a marshmallow on a skewer over an open flame — we were stranded. Right there on the side of a busy interstate. I remained in my damp nightgown, holding an even damper pillowcase. The bulk of my clothing had increased due to them being covered in ditch water, so not only was I feeling my feet on the cold, rocky asphalt, but now I was carrying a soggy pillowcase containing the only belongings I had left to my name. The coldness of the night increased with each car that passed by. Their motion pushed an invisible blast of freezing air against my wet sticky body.

Wanda insisted to the officers that a bomb was the cause of the explosion and that she was now being hunted. With one external combustion, several were set off inside her head. She had become the prey…She believed Johnny and his new woman wanted to take her out or had Huff and Joker learned she reported the murder of the unsuspecting hiker to Secret Witness?

At one point, she was fed up with them dominating Johnny's time and found a way to get rid of them. I remember standing next to her in a phone booth with cracked glass when she called. She had held onto the Hiker's wallet with his identification card inside. I detected a moment of softness as Wanda spoke to the person on the other end of the line. I knew she made the call to get rid of Huff and Joker, but somewhere during the conversation, I sensed Wanda was proud of herself for doing the right thing. At least, I wanted to believe that. I wanted to believe deep inside she felt bad for the young hiker who was thrown off a cliff for no reason. No reason other than he was trying to be a good guy while on his journey.

It didn't matter now. Now Wanda believed Huff and Joker had possibly put a hit out on her from inside a prison cell. Or was it the robbers wearing the ski masks? She had a list of potential assassins running around inside her mind, and like the explosion, they were popping off like a mouth full of Pop Rocks.

"Ma'am, we won't know the cause of the fire until the investigation is complete," said an overweight officer while staring her right in the eyes. "I can say it again, but that's the bottom line," he continued. "In the meantime, why don't we take y'all back to the town you came from, so you can get your kids to bed, huh?" This self-confident middle-aged officer with a burly mustache had no idea we didn't have a bed. Wanda had only returned to the blue house with the fancy door to collect a few things after the robbery, which was pointless because they were now gone too.

Help! Don't leave me with her! I wanted to shout and pound my fists like she had the night we were robbed. I envisioned myself slowly walking over to one of the police cars and letting myself inside. I started to experience something I hadn't known before, hopelessness. I no longer believed my life would get better. I no longer believed I would have a normal mom and dad. Nor that I, Vicki, and Lee would have a tire swing hanging from a large oak tree in our backyard and a tree fort like we dreamed of. I also knew that even if we did get a tire swing and a tree fort, it wouldn't be long before it would be ripped out from underneath us.

Nothing lasted with Wanda. *This is it..., this is what I've got..., and this is my life...* I told myself. My spirit drifted somewhere far away as my soul descended into a gloomy state.

"I need witness protection," Wanda yelled. "Protection from who?" the pudgy officer appeared puzzled and a little annoyed... "Someone is after me. Can't you fucking see that!? "Okay, I'm going to ask one last time," his volume increased — "Where can we escort you and your kids too?" My sister Diana chose to return to her apartment with her girls as Wanda chose to get us a lift to the next town south. It was about another 45 minutes away. Ninety miles from where we lived, from the grandparents' house, Sycamore Elementary, and from Annie. However, the distance between us would end up feeling like we lived on separate planets.

I arrived in the unfamiliar town in which we would reside in the back seat of a black and white carriage with bars and bright blue and red flashing lights. Would this be my Cinderella story? We landed at a rundown off-white motel. It reminded me of the motel in a scary movie I had watched with my older sisters. One in which a man slaughtered women while they were showering and spent his spare time dressing up like his mother.

However, this motel was taller and had a single row of front doors on the bottom floor. It was late, very late now. Wanda led us inside while the officer split as fast as he appeared. I observed our new home. There was a bed in the living area, and off to the far corner was a small bathroom with a shower. It had yucky blue broken tile, but the faucet ran warm. I was grateful. Back out in the main room, I spotted a back door which I thought was odd to have inside a motel room and I quickly made my way over to it — aroused by wonder. I was shocked by another surprise when I got to the door, to my left, there was a narrow stairwell that was held together by two concrete walls. Should I see what's on the other side of the door or go upstairs first?

I called to Vicki and Lee, "look what I found," and howled like a werewolf as I placed the soles of my feet on the first step. I belted up the narrow staircase as they climbed behind me. "Where wee are go'in Jade?" Lee asked with wide eyes. He was so cute and young. "We are inside a magical lighthouse Mr. Lee. I wonder what we will find...?" I cheekily replied with a mischievous smile while pretending to speak into a microphone.

I was shocked to see a full-size bed with a wooden nightstand holding a simple lamp when we reached the top. There were no windows, and the ceiling hung low, but surely

I, Vicki, and Lee could all fit into the bed. I jumped on top of the bed, "Yay…We have entered into the Great Lantern Room," I joyfully exclaimed. And although I was glad to learn we had our own space, on the inside, I wasn't as ecstatic as I was pretending to be. A new friend named Cloud of Black Hopelessness entered my life, but I would hide and pretend to see Vicki and Lee smile. I wanted to conceal the truth about our real life from them as long as I could.

We ran back down the stairs exploring the other rooms inside our lighthouse. We went to the back door and opened it. Startled, I took a shallow breath and held it. My eyes were wide open like Lee's had been earlier. As I slowly opened the door, a cold, sharp breeze crept into the motel room. Descending stairs appeared beneath me while the aroma of wet rocks hit my nostrils. I wondered if there could be a mossy pond at the bottom of the stairs. It was too dark to see anything except the first few steps…a room possessed by an absence of light. Wanda had gone to find a pay phone. I wasn't sure if I should venture down the stairs but was way too curious not to. While my fingers grappled on a damp stone wall, I found a light switch.

I turned it on and told Vicki and Lee to stay inside as I lightly tiptoed down the rickety stairs. When I arrived at the bottom, I realized it was an old basement turned kitchen, but it wasn't even the typical type. There was an oversized fridge covered in rust, and on an old worktable set a two-burner hotplate. There was no oven, no table and chairs, and no warmth. It felt like a car garage carved out of rocks. There was a dim light bulb that hung from the patched seepage ceiling. I quickly imagined how dark it would be inside our new kitchen if that light bulb burned out. Chills went up my spine as I imagined it would be like my Dad's crawlspace, only larger, like a dungeon. Had Wanda the Wicked Dragon finally been led to her dark dungeon? If so, why did I have to be here? Why couldn't I be somewhere else? I didn't want this new home. Shivering, I met Vicki and Lee at the top of the stairs and closed the door behind me. I didn't like that room. There was something about it that sent demonic chills throughout my body. It was hard to brush off like an unseen spider web. I could feel it, but I couldn't see it.

Upon Wanda's return, her face drooped, and she wore a noticeable frown. Gone was her bold confidence, gone was her Johnny, her drugs, and her money, but most importantly — gone was the power she believed she had. At that moment, I wanted to comfort her, but my body forbade it.

After a warm shower, I headed up to my new room with Vicki and Lee tiptoeing behind me. I was relieved to have a bed to crawl into, even though I had to encourage several cockroaches to find a new home when I pulled back the sheets. They scurried to the edges of the bed like the red sea parting, and I opted to sleep with the light on to let them know I could see them...I was tired, too tired to care. I was grateful to be warm and dry, but there was no denying how drained I was from the night, and not even a thousand cockroaches were going to deter me from climbing into that bed.

However, as I laid there looking at the ceiling I could almost reach, I was still acutely aware of my newfound awakening. The awakening of the fact that my body spoke to me, that it warned me of danger. That I wasn't always looking around for no reason. There was a reason, and now I understood that reason.

The little Sparrow's wings were widening. She was growing up way too fast, but she had to in order to survive the storms. She had found confidence in knowledge, and even though the Black Cloud of Hopelessness would attempt to hover over her and rob her of all the freedoms other young birds enjoyed — she decided somewhere deep inside herself that she would fight the robber of her joy and that she would, one day, find freedom.

Chapter Eleven
The Basement

Summer moved abruptly into the valley with a blistering blaze. One day Wanda took us to the nearest thrift store. I was able to find a pair of sandals with soles barely worn. Since the fire, we had become vagabonds who pounded the pavement — walking everywhere we needed to go.

As we strolled through the town, set on bluffs splattered with red dirt, we passed by a large cathedral and could see the bell tower. I was drawn to the cathedral, and I wanted to go inside, but Wanda refused. Settling into our new life on the Bluffs had been extremely challenging. I dreaded the thought of starting a new school in the state in which we were. I usually feared starting a new school. But this was different — this town smelled of money, and that was something we didn't have.

I began attending school at Bluff Heights Elementary, and just as I had apprehended, no one reached out to be my friend. My days there were lonely. I was the last student to be chosen to play on teams during P.E. I hated standing there while the popular kids scanned the group and slowly plucked everyone but me.

Refusal mocked me with every student picked before me, and as they crossed the field — what I already knew was reinforced repeatedly. How I longed for Annie's big smile and friendship. I shook off the memories of Bluff Heights Elementary, thankful my time there had ended.

Wanda was able to make it to the welfare office soon after we carved out a new hole to live in and began receiving food stamps and money. We had our white bread and cheese sandwiches once again. Wanda would even go down into her dragon's pit to make us French toast sometimes.

Wanda learned there were churches in town that gave out free dinners, but you had to eat there. So, inside a small church with a tall steeple, we'd sit at a table while a preacher gave a sermon towards the end of each month. I liked it there. It wasn't like at school. My ragged clothes didn't seem to matter to the kids there. Many of which looked like they shopped at the same secondhand store, except for the pastors' kids and other kids who came with their parents to serve us.

I was so comfortable there that I'd forget we were there for the food amongst people who slept on the sidewalks. There were a few other kids who ate at the church who seemed to speak my language, which was refreshing. We knew things other children our age didn't know. It was nice not having to pretend, but unlike some of them, I wanted a different life. I knew one day I would escape my cage and do something better. I would never be like my mom or dad.

There was another thing I had come to enjoy — behind the office lived the owners of the motel. They were from a country called India. Divya was the mom. She was beautiful and dressed in magical clothing. She looked like a real-life princess. And even though she was quiet, she had an inviting spirit like Annie's mom. I felt warmth extended to me when I entered her space. Divya had two children, Kiara and Darsh. Kiara was my age, and Darsh was a few years older. We became fast friends. Besides the dinners at the church, they were my happiness while I played in purgatory.

Wanda was off the white powder, but she was still mean. She still talked to me like she hated me, but I was comforted when she started cuddling and singing silly little songs with Vicki and Lee. Why didn't she cuddle with me, though? Was it because I remembered? Was it because she remembered when she looked at me? Was there a part of her that felt bad about the things that she had done?

She was financially broke, and even with her tooth fixed, she lacked all the fancy things she enjoyed. One day I sat across from her as she watched tv while holding Lee in her arms and decided to draw a picture of her because, at that moment, she looked loving and soft — she looked like a nice mommy. Her long blonde hair glistened, and her green eyes sparkled.

I sat adjacent to her and drew a picture of her face, a kind face, a loving face, a face like a mother's. Something had moved my heart to make Wanda a gift. It had been a long time since the broken glass. I wanted to make an effort to reach her. Maybe there was still an ever so slight chance that she would hold me too.

I abruptly jumped up when I finished the picture and flipped on the light. "What are you doing, Jade? I'm watching 60 minutes," she snapped. "Mom, I made you something," I said while shrugging my shoulders with a tender smile. "Yeah, what's that, Jade?" She seemed bothered, but I was brave and approached her. I had done a really good job...I wanted her to see how I saw her at that moment. A moment of a possible truce.

If nothing else, she would surely appreciate that I thought she was pretty. "What's this?" she asked as I handed her the portrait. "It's you, mom. I drew a picture of you holding Lee."

"For crying out loud, that doesn't fucking look like me. My eyes aren't squinty like that, and my lips aren't big like that. I'm not black....!" She screamed while looking at it again. "You little fucking snake, I'll kill you, Jade, you evil bitch" she threw Lee off her lap. Screaming at the top of her lungs while standing over me, she ripped the picture. The pieces fell like snowflakes floating to the bottom of a snow globe.

Screeching, her hand flew across my cheek, followed by both hands grabbing my hair on each side of my head. She pulled my head back and forth repeatedly. I felt like my scalp was being ripped from my head. I cried and pleaded with her to let go. Vicki and Lee began to scream, "STOP STOP hurting Jade, mommy…" She let go, I dropped to the floor.

I continued to lay there with tears soaking the floor beneath my face as I heard the front door slam.

I was just trying to be nice, but instead of a hug, I got hit. I slowly stood up and collected the pieces of the portrait I had drawn, along with some miscellaneous wrappers, and put them into the trash.

That evening I put myself, Vicky, and Lee to bed. I didn't know where Wanda had gone, and I hated being inside that motel room alone at night, but they needed sleep, and so did I. In the middle of the night, I started to have a nightmare. I was held down by demons, I couldn't move, and in my nightmare, everything was dark. I couldn't see anything except evil eyes staring at me. The pressure from their force pinned me to my bed. I tried to scream for God to help me, but no words would come out of my mouth. The pressure on my eyes made it hard to peel them back just enough to see evil glaring back at me. In my nightmare, I was finally able to let out a scream which pushed against the unseen power.

"God, God help!" I wailed... Finally, I awoke, feeling remnants of the force that pinned me down to the bed. Terror ran through my veins. I tried to turn the little light on that sat on the nightstand. Why was it off? I frantically turned the knob, but the bulb was toast. Then I remembered the cockroaches. Were they under my feet? Were they crawling on me? I envisioned them glued to my t-shirt and shorts.

It was dark, just like in my nightmare. I felt the concrete walls on both sides of my hands as I made my way down the stairwell. Making my way into the main room. I flipped on the light. When it came on it was revealed that Wanda was still gone. I looked at the clock flashing 3:00 AM. Where was Wanda? I wondered where she had gone as I watched roaches make their way into hiding.

Why did the picture make her so mad? Angry enough to leave us all night? Was she out doing drugs? Had she met someone new? Would she return, or was this it? Was this going to be the time that she never came back? I couldn't fall back to sleep. I didn't feel safe, and I had to make sure that no one broke in and that Vicki and Lee would remain safe.

I did a few rounds to make sure the doors were locked and sat down on the bed. Glancing over at the notepad and the colored pencils, I decided to throw them into the trash basket along with the pieces of the portrait. Eventually, Vicki and Lee woke up, but there was still no sign of Wanda. I wasn't sure I wanted her to return, but I acknowledged the fact that I felt a form of protection when she was there and realized that in her absence my only covering was gone.

She eventually emerged smelling of pot and liquor. Wanda hadn't been a big drinker like dad, but when she did drink, it usually led to other things. "You guys hungry?" she asked. "No, I made us some cereal," I responded. She nodded her head and proceeded to the shower. I knew the bars didn't stay open all night, so I assumed Wanda had most likely met someone new and had a little rendezvous.

I thought she would be sorry when she returned to the motel. I thought maybe she would show some compassion for hitting me or apologize for ripping up the picture I drew for her, but she gave nothing to me except an emotionless node. My hurt turned to anger. I hated her. I hated who she was, and I hated that she was my mom. She would never change or love me, but why?

It wasn't long before Wanda started bringing her new friend around. He liked to drink. He didn't get mean and violent like my dad, but they got slushy together and would lock lips in front of us until their passionate lust led them upstairs. Wanda adopted the upstairs room after she met Wesley.

Which I hated even more than the feeling I got when he came around. I also hated sleeping near the basement door. The basement's creepiness lurked behind that door. Wes was another young guy. He looked like he could have been her son. He wore tight Levis and a gold chain. He wasn't the typical type of guy Wanda picked. Perhaps it was simply for attention and to fulfill her sexual needs. It certainly wasn't because he could provide food for us.

We spent a lot of time hungry during that season. Some days, Wanda would go without eating so that we could. Possibly, due to some fear, she would be reported for starving us to death, or it could have been a mustard seed of love?

It started to heat up. The temperature in the valley was rising, and the motel room only had a small swamp cooler. We had a pool which was great because I was able to swim with Kiara and Darsh. And sometimes, at night, we would collect June Bugs off the sidewalks and tie them to a string until they made a loud buzzing sound.

Kiara and Darsh didn't get to go to the park with me or down by the river. They had gone to a different school too. I would trade them my peanut butter and honey sandwiches for Kati rolls, but they didn't tell their parents. Kiara and Darsh had strict parents who watched them very closely and cared a lot about their grades.

I began to leave Vicki and Lee alone with Wanda and Wes more often to hang out with them. I felt guilty, but Vicki and Lee still couldn't swim, and Vicki had started to tell on me. I still adored her and understood she was sad because I had new friends and was seeking attention from Wanda.

One afternoon, Wanda announced she, Wes, and Lee were going for a walk. I was confused. Why wouldn't they take Vicki and me? Or at least Vicki…It was muggy inside the room, so I stood in front of the swamp cooler to get some air. It was cooler inside the basement, but I dreaded going down there. I couldn't get used to it. I wondered if someone had been murdered, and I was picking up on an atmosphere of tragedy.

I heard a knock at the door. Who's here, I wondered. I couldn't even peek out the door without opening it, and there wasn't a window I could look through. "Hello, Jade, you in there? Your mom asked me to bring you and your sister some sodas." I opened the door to find a man standing there I had never seen before. He wore a baseball cap and reeked of cologne.

"Hey Jade, I'm your Mom and Wesley's friend," he said as he pushed his way inside, carrying a six-pack of soda. He broke one off and handed it to me with a friendly smile. "Thank you," I said under my breath. "Hey, do you have somewhere cool we can keep these?" I noticed he peeked over at Vicki in a way that made me uneasy. Vicki was sleeping. "Well, do you have a place where we can keep these cold?" he asked again.

"Sure," I reluctantly replied as I opened up the basement door and led him down the stairs. "Wow, this is a really trippy room," he said. I walked over to the fridge as he followed closely behind me and held open the door as he flung the sodas inside. Letting the heavy door close itself, I quickly headed towards the stairs.

"You're prettier than your mom said," I heard him say from behind me...*What the hell? I am not even a teenager.* I thought. My thick strawberry-blonde hair had made its way to my lower back, but I didn't look older for my age. I didn't wear makeup, had no boobs, and he looked like a normal guy — he could have even passed for a cop.

He didn't look like the drug addicts Wanda had left me with before. The ones who fondled me in the dark or Uncle

Pete with his weird tick. He was dressed nicely and smelled good. He was clean-cut and didn't have any tattoos. What was he doing? Why was he here? I turned around as I was backing up and mustered up enough courage to tell him to stay away from me.

He smiled like he had just won a prize at the carnival. "Wait, Jade, it's okay, really." I headed for the stairs, but before I could even get to the bottom step, he grabbed me. "It's okay, it won't hurt, and I don't want to hurt you, Jade," he said. "I really don't want to hurt you, sweet girl." I closed my eyes as he ran both his hands down my hair. My eyes were closed, but I could feel him smiling. I thought of Vicki sleeping upstairs and prayed she wouldn't wake. I usually knew the men who molested me, but I had never seen this man before.

I stood silent as he put his hands up my shirt and began to kiss my face. I smelled a mixture of spearmint gum and alcohol. He pressed himself against me. I could feel his hardness. I became more aware of what might happen to Vicki if she woke. Something about this guy told me he could turn cold fast. I unzipped his pants and found him. "That's it, that's a good girl," he moaned with shallow breaths. I wanted to please him, so he would go away. Would it be enough? Or would he want more? He began to jerk as he relieved himself all over my face. Wiping my mouth, I felt sick.

"You're a dirty little thing," he said as he zipped up his pants with a clown-like smile. *No, I'm not. You're the dirty one, you freak.* I wanted to tell him what I thought, but I knew better. Vicki was right upstairs, and we were still in a dark basement.

"You know the rules, right?" he asked. I didn't know his rules, but I assumed they were the same rules everyone else had. Don't tell anyone, or they will just think your lying, or if you tell anyone, I'll kill you and your family, starting with your baby brother. I shook my head yes as he kissed my forehead while he fondled my private area once last time before sprinting up the stairs and making his way out the front door.

I was confused. Who was that guy, and where was Wanda? Shortly after he left, she returned with Lee. She had a bag full of groceries, and I noticed she was wearing new lipstick and a hat. Where did she get that money? We had no money, and it was the end of the month. She looked over at me and said, "Why don't you go play outside or something."

"Mom, some guy came here and said he knew you and Wes. He was strange and brought sodas." "Ya, I know Jade, how do you think he knew how to get here, duh?" Her words hit me like a hammer in the gut. She had sent him to me! And to my little sister for money to get food, lipstick, and a new hat. It hadn't been the typical molestation after all. Wanda had become the madam of her 10-year-old daughter, me.

The Sparrow's soul shattered into a thousand pieces. The arrow went straight through her heart. Her wound bled profusely, but her heart would continue to beat.

Chapter Twelve
SOS

I felt changed by my new knowledge more so than by the sexual encounters I experienced. Something inside me died when I learned my mom had sold me for groceries, lipstick, and a hat. I walked around dazed and confused, and although I might have looked like me and talked like me, I was no longer fully me. I was the robot version of myself again, only hollower and angrier. I distanced myself from Vicki and Lee. I was left in their charge often, but playful interaction was snipped, cut, and downloaded into a secret place. Pretending to be astronauts flying to the moon or pretending to be a teacher handing them tasks was no longer on my radar. My drive to see their smile was deeply submerged underneath a blanket of numbness. I still loved them dearly, but walls enclosed around my heart like the ancient city of Jericho, and it would take God himself to bring them down.

I had told myself Wanda had been bad because of the white powder (the meth) and the prison gang, but now I realized it wasn't those things. She wasn't on meth, and no Peckerwoods had come around. I wondered if she knew about other things too. Did she know about the other men who molested me? Did she arrange some of those too? Did she know about the time I protected Vicki from a man she left us with in a dirty motel room by giving him myself when I was eight? I remembered a fight between her and Diana one day in which Diana yelled at her for selling her to a man who made her watch him "jerk off" all day for a box full of new hats and a fur jacket. Had that really happened!? Now it was my turn? A tsunami of questions consumed me. I had moments of wanting to die before, but I really wanted to die now.

Men continued to visit me inside that motel room, inside the basement, and sometimes inside their own homes. It was hard to look Kiara and Darsh in the eyes anymore. They were so innocent, loved, and treasured. Darsh was older than me, but he would have never imagined what was going on. How could I tell him? How could I tell anyone? I was the bump in Wanda's paycheck which provided extra food and clothing. I would have preferred to be bumped into a ditch somewhere and left for dead. I thought of my dad occasionally and began to get angry at him too. I strongly disliked drunk Gary, but why didn't he come to look for me? He was still my dad, and he wasn't always drunk. When he was sober, he was pretty cool. We'd go to the river and have rock skipping competitions. He'd make me laugh with silly jokes. And sometimes, we'd sit in a circle on the front lawn with his friends and share the milk from a cracked coconut. Even when he fried on acid, he treated me better than Wanda, and I was starting to feel like I could stand up to Uncle Pete. Uncle Pete was nothing compared to some of the men I met that summer.

I started spending as much time as I could away from the motel. I would go to the river alone and made a swing at the park, my second home. Sometimes I walked the cobblestone path alongside the water and imagined jumping in and being swept away by the currents. The walk back to the motel always felt long and dreadful. Even though, sometimes I wished it would have never ended. Could I just keep going? Would my body become so fatigued it would simply stop working? Sometimes I was so tired I considered sleeping on the sidewalk or at the park, but when darkness approached, my mind waged war with those thoughts, and in the end, I returned to what I knew.

Gone was the playful me who had hopes and dreams and a wild imagination. I awoke each morning in a somber state. The Cloud of Black Hopelessness was my daily companion as I walked through a dark tunnel called, "My Life." I no longer heard from the helper. That whisper was silenced. I no longer prayed for God to help me, but I kept a Bible I got from the food church underneath my pillow each night. I believed it would keep the nightmares away, but they would still come and invade my sleep. Yet, it was my comfort. I would often wake in horror, but instead of running to a safe mommy or daddy, I would grab my Bible and rest my face on it, something about it felt protective.

One afternoon, while Wanda and Wesley were at the river drinking, I headed into the basement to eat when I looked over and saw a pair of kitchen shears on the makeshift countertop. I thought of how much Wanda hated short hair on females and would often reference them as "dikes." I grabbed the shears and marched up the stairs. The basement no longer scared me. Now it was only a fat belly full of scars.

I drifted towards the fluorescent glow coming from the little bathroom carrying the kitchen shears. Looking at my reflection, staring into my deep blue eyes, I wondered who I was. "Who are you, Jade?" I asked myself. I saw my round face, my rosy cheeks, and my pouty full lips. I saw my long wavy hair. I was told I looked like my dad's biological father, who I had never met. His grandparents traveled to America from Ireland. I had a different look about me than my siblings, and neither looked like my mom or dad.

I grabbed a handful of my hair, brought the shears to it, and cut it. I would cut all my hair off, I decided. It was the one thing people told me was pretty about me. I didn't want to be pretty. Not now. Not here in this rotten room. I didn't care if Wanda beat me or made fun of me. I hoped she would hate what I had done. I kept cutting off bulks of my hair, rapidly accelerating my pace until my hair ended right below my ears. I dropped the kitchen shears in the sink and gazed into my eyes again. I investigated a look inside them I hadn't seen before, a look like Wanda and Gary's when they were mad. I then turned my gaze to the remains of my hair, which now covered the broken tile and put it into the trash. Leaving the shears in the sink with the old me, I left the motel room.

I roamed the streets that day, looking like I had just escaped from a third-world country orphanage. Staying far away from the river, from Wanda, Wesley, Vicki, and Lee. People would look at me as they passed by, and although their expressions told a thousand stories — no one said a word. No one cared.

I stopped in front of the large cathedral with the bell tower. I felt drawn to what was on the other side of the large bronze-looking doors. It wasn't like the vibe I used to get, which lurked behind the basement door, it was a pull, an intrigue, a curiosity. Wanda wasn't there to stop me this time. Was God inside there? Is that why she didn't want to go inside? I made my way up to the handle, which looked like it had been made for a giant's hand. I pulled with all my might, but the door wouldn't open. I tried the other, but it was locked too. I exhausted myself in disappointment as I repeatedly tried to open the large doors, but they wouldn't budge. I turned my back to the doors that turned their back on me just as a bird landed a few feet from me.

It was a little pudgy buffy-brown bird with stripes on its back. I looked into the bird's eyes — we held our gaze. It didn't look away like most birds. It was saying, "Hello, I see you. No one else wanted to say hello, but I do. Don't lose heart. Hold on. I want to play with you. One day you will be free like me." The little bird hopped over to my shoe and pecked it, I didn't move. I didn't want it to go away. A smile snuck its way across my face as something moved inside my chest. I heard myself gently laugh as the little bird turned and flew away.

The Sparrow survived by apathetically riding the waves of her life, which continually smashed her into the seafloor. The force of the water would finally wash her ashore, leaving her to dry and giving her moments to recover from the wounds she endured.

Chapter Thirteen
Rescued

My new boy cut didn't detour the men as I had hoped and only gave Wanda something to mock. The handful of regulars continued. Wanda would even thank them and have long talks with them in front of me. It was as if she had found new friends in them. Wesley also knew them, fist-pumped them, and laughed with them. Who were these people? A circle of perverts who danced in the rain of a little girl's pain? Were they the demons from my nightmares dressed in clothes?

Wesley and Wanda had become quite a pair. They spent most of their time getting high and drinking at the river. When they didn't do that, they went shopping. Wanda was saving for a car but would take from the car savings to buy cigarettes for Wesley and anything else they decided to get.

The school was going to start soon at Bluff Heights Elementary. Wanda told me she'd buy me new school clothes this year and a new backpack as soon as she bought a car. My stomach ached when I remembered the kids at that school, but I thought about how new clothes might help me get a friend or at least be invited to join a team during PE. I also thought about how being at school would help me stay away from the motel, Wanda and Wesley.

It was smoldering hot one day inside our room but even hotter outside. The dust and dirt from the valley floor created wind tunnels that swirled and danced along the red dirt. It was miserable. I sat as close as I could get to the little swamp cooler that was in the wall underneath the one window we had in the main room, but my clothes still stuck to me like there was a layer of school glue between them and me. I was startled by a loud knock at the door. Wanda and Wesley were startled too. Wanda had her head on Wesley's lap recovering from a hangover from the night before, and a vampire movie played on tv.

"Wanda Sue, you in there?" I heard a man's voice ask. His voice was authoritative, controversial, and deep. He began to thump ferociously on the door. "Wanda Sue, open up this fucking door now. I hear you in there, it's George, open the door now, Wanda," he shouted. "I will break it down, damn it," he continued. Wanda sat up and aimed for the door. Opening it, she threw her arms around the man ignoring the gun he held in his hand. He quickly looked at me before pushing Wanda aside and pointed his gun at Wesley.

"Get up," he demanded. "Get your shit and get out of here. If you ever come around my sister or these kids again, I'll blow your fucking head off like the fucking cockroach you are." The fierce man watched as Wesley wiggled passed him and slithered out the door. "Wanda, get your kids, let's go." "Go where George?" she asked. "Look around, you're in a shithole. Get your kids, and let's go now." "I need to grab a few things." "There's nothing from here you need," he asserted.

Who was this man, I wondered...*George*? Was this the Uncle George I had heard Wanda brag about my whole life? The one who accidentally shot my aunt in the head when Wanda's dad gave him a rifle on his 15th birthday. The one who joined the Navy and became an oil engineer overseas. The eldest of all of Georgia's children. The one who had cared for Wanda, the baby of the family, until he was forced to leave due to Georgia's inability to forgive his mistake.

He squatted down next to me as I stayed frozen in place. "Are you Jade?" he asked. I nodded my head in response. "Get up, sweetheart, you're coming with me," he said as he placed his hand on my cheek. His eyes were the shade of mine, but thousands of daggers swam inside them. However, none were aimed at me. Something inside me understood I was being rescued by a man I had never met before. By one of Wanda's legends, only this legend looked true and real and had his hand on my cheek. He had come to take us away from the rotten room, from the basement, from the men. How did he know? Who told him?

He escorted us out the door and led us down the small path leading to the parking lot. Speechless, we trailed behind him — following him closely like a guide on an unfamiliar outing. Other than the purse Wanda carried, we took nothing. Leaving with just the clothes on our backs. We approached a brand-new blue Cadillac. It even had a keypad with the secret code on the door, which Uncle George punched in before opening all the doors for us. I slid into the back seat along with Vicki and Lee and slid across the blue leather upholstery. It was the most beautiful car I had ever been inside. When the atmosphere thinned and things calmed down, Uncle George shared with us the different parts he had custom-made for his Cadillac.

He shared with us some of his journeys overseas and told us of how he married a woman who was born and raised in Venezuela. A woman who he had met in Saudi Arabia while working the oil fields. Her name was Betty, a name she gave herself when they traveled to America. Uncle George went on to share with us that he had called Grandma Georgia to ask about us; she told him that all she knew was that we were staying at a rundown motel room in the valley, and she told him of the things she feared concerning Wanda. Uncle George and his wife decided to leave Saudi Arabia and make their way back to America so Uncle George could make his way to us.

I didn't know where we were going, but I believed it would be somewhere better. I heard Uncle George tell Wanda how he had a fully furnished house waiting for us, how the Cadillac would be hers to use, and how he had been searching for us. I had never known a man like this. He spoke like a tough guy like most of the Peckerwoods had, but he was different. Something inside my gut told me he could be more dangerous than them, but he was classy and well spoken. He even spoke other languages, and on his car radio, he played music in a dialect I had never heard.

We drove for several hours, stopping to eat inside a real restaurant. I had a cheeseburger, french fries, and a vanilla milkshake. Uncle George told me to order anything I wanted, and I didn't hesitate to do so. I hung onto every word he said. A monstrous admiration for my uncle bloomed into a full-grown tree before we even arrived at our new house. His stories mesmerized me. Uncle George didn't hold back any details when he spoke. He told us how he had gained lots of wealth overseas and had even dined with the princes of Saudi Arabia.

Eventually, we arrived at our destination. Sitting before us was a spacious garden tract home. The driveway was paved with red bricks, which climbed up the sides of the house. There was a large garage and a timber frame entryway. It was beautiful, like the Cadillac. I followed behind my talkative Uncle, who verged on the edge of being a braggart, but I liked him. Wanda was as timid as a mouse in his presence and spoke like someone I didn't know, and I liked that too.

I picked up on the scent of a lumber mill nearby as we entered the house, or was it all the exposed wood? I didn't ask, nor did I care—the house was perfect. It was a dream. The carpet was white, and I spotted a red velvet couch right away with a mahogany table sitting in front of it. There were area rugs as I had never seen before. They were black with gold swirls and subtle colors throughout. There was a large dining table and cushions on the chairs. Uncle George seemed to focus on me as much as I focused on him. When he spoke, his eyes included me in every conversation.

He gestured for me to follow him down the hall. Vicki and Lee were right behind me. He pointed to one of the rooms, "Jade, this room is for you and your sister," he said. I went inside to discover bunk beds. I had never had bunk beds before. There was a simple but elegant chest that stood on four legs pushed up against the wall with blankets neatly folded on top. White sheer drapes with red roses imprinted on them hung beautifully over a large window. A tall mahogany dresser that almost seemed to reach the ceiling sat on the other side of the room. Children's books were perfectly placed inside a basket on the floor next to it.

We then followed him into what would be Wanda's room. I realized Uncle George knew her favorite color was yellow when I spotted a stunning yellow hand-embroidered quilt on top of a queen Victorian-style bed. Then we went to the third room, which Uncle George explained would be his for now, but later would be Lee's. He said he would be sleeping on the twin-size bed he had bought for Lee until all the "riff raff" stayed away. He had a doorknob with a lock on it to that room and a deadbolt above that. He said he would hold the only key so that we children did not mess around with that room.

117

Uncle George didn't seem to notice my hair, my ugliness, but he seemed to see me. I felt like he looked right through me and knew everything. I wondered if he knew what Wanda had done too but loved her anyway. I didn't know or understand what made this man tick, but the one thing I did know was that my new savior had stolen my heart and gained my respect within one drive and entry into a new life.

The Sparrow was led to a luxurious nest by a courageous, brave legend she had only heard about. She took it all in as the courage in her DNA began to speak again. She felt life rushing through her veins like a raging river. Hope was alive again. The Sparrow was rescued— at least for now...

Chapter Fourteen
Aunt Betty

The first night in my new bed was glorious. I got the top bunk, and Vicki picked the bottom, so that worked out perfectly. I was startled awake several times to remember what had transpired. Knowing Uncle George was in the next room brought me mountains of comfort, even though I barely knew him. I trusted him. I had heard good things about him my whole life, not from Grandma Georgia or from my Aunt Junie, but from Wanda. Uncle George was an atheist (he didn't believe in God), Grandma Georgia told me. That tacked onto the shooting of my aunt left my uncle without a supportive mother of his own. I thought about how we had that in common. How Georgia didn't like him and how Wanda didn't like me. And I thought about how he was sleeping in the room next to mine and how different it was that I felt safe with him doing so. I knew with every fiber of my being he wasn't like those other men or Uncle Pete. When I thought about how he had a room full of guns and would use them to protect me—my chest would inflate with courage forcing me to stand straighter and breathe deeper. I felt taller; he empowered me. He taught me how to handle guns, starting with an Uzi propped up on a pillow while sitting on the red velvet couch. He mirrored an intensely focused sniper getting ready to pull the trigger when he taught me about its components. His every action, his every word, made it clear that he was on a mission to save his "baby sister" and her kids.

I rarely spoke to Wanda. There was a 25-foot glass wall separating us. We could see and feel each other, but there was a barrier between us. I imagined maybe one day, when I grew older, she might slither up that wall, peek over, and have a good look at my life. I knew she was NOT the person I saw her pretending to be around Uncle George. I knew who she was, and I would never trust her. I hated everything about her. When she acted nicely, my contempt intensified. Her voice sounded like chalk screeching across a blackboard. She started chewing gum all the time. She smacked her lips and popped bubbles sucking air between her teeth afterward. Disgust inched its way up onto the surface of my scalp like murky water, seeped out, and drizzled down my body poking and prodding my every nerve. Her very presence was an excruciating form of torture.

I no longer craved or longed for her to hug me, but the thought of her touching me repelled me from even getting close to her. She started cooking again, which I did enjoy because she cooked really good. My willpower failed me completely when I smelled her fried chicken searing in oil, and I made my way to the kitchen. However, I made sure she was aware I was sitting as far away from her as possible while I ate. She also prepared sweets from scratch, baked apple pies, and made persimmon cookies from our own persimmon tree.

I eventually got to meet Aunt Betty and fell in love with her immediately. She didn't have any children and seemed to take a liking to me. She was short and a little on the plump side but attractive. She spoke with an accent and, like Uncle George, could speak several different languages. She enjoyed showing me pictures of herself overseas when she was younger. She looked beautiful in her pictures—I found her beautiful still. She was classy and liked nice things, but not in a way like Wanda. Aunt Betty was strong, smart, well mannered and sophisticated. I understood she was sacrificing time with my uncle while he spent his days and nights with us. Uncle George didn't want Aunt Betty to visit our home because he thought we might be in some sort of danger. However, I learned before our arrival that she had furnished the house for us. She was the one who bought and placed the children's books perfectly inside the basket for Vicki and me. She bought us the delicate white sheer drapes covered in red roses for our room and chose bunkbeds to give us "more space."

She didn't have any family in America. Her father owned a large construction company that operated in Saudi Arabia. Aunt Betty had been his head accountant and ran the company office when she met my uncle. However, most of her family still resided in Venezuela. I enjoyed listening to her talk with her family. She intrigued me. She didn't seem to take such a liking to Vicki and Lee but would take me shopping and even took me to get my hair professionally done. We had one thing in common, something that seemed to bond us from the beginning: neither of us liked Wanda. She did not like having Wanda at her home, but she would have me. It was revealed by the things she said that she had sacrificed her relationship with her father for my uncle and us children. If it had been strictly for Wanda, she would "have stayed in Saudi."

Aunt Betty became my teacher for all things lovely. She taught me about the importance of education. She explained how education could break cycles of dysfunction. I did not fully understand the concept of "cycles," but I understood that she was teaching me that I could be different than Wanda. That if I did good in school, I could one day go to college and buy a new home for myself. She told me that "no one could ever take away my education." She shared with me how her dad had paid for her to have a private tutor when she was growing up and how she had made a lot of her own money. She said she would get me a private tutor, too, if I needed extra help.

I was thrilled to start school that year. I would be going into the sixth grade. It would be different this time. I had a nice home, my aunt and uncle, and NO ONE would know about the basement or me. I wasn't accustomed to having friends over, but I flirted with the thought. I dreamed of making friends, going to birthday parties, and one day maybe having one of my very own.

Uncle George stuck to us like glue. He drove Wanda to enroll us in school. Traced the bus route and bought me the best backpack full of supplies. Aunt Betty bought me not one but two brand-new pairs of shoes for school. She said one pair was to wear with the dresses, which frightened me slightly, and the sneakers were to wear with jeans and sweats. She then went on to remind me several times to always take my shoes off when I got home and to put my old ones on. She also bought house slippers for us all and taught me how to keep carpets clean by taking our shoes off at the door. I admired everything about her. Somehow, she and Uncle George managed to seep through the walls around my heart.

I was still plagued by nightmares. They continued to invade my sleep...One night, while asleep, I envisioned there was a knock at the door. When Wanda opened it, there was a man standing there. He pointed his index finger right at her face and boldly said, "You Are The Witch..." After that, when she swept the kitchen floor, I would imagine her face turning green and her flying out the door on her broomstick to find her flock of fleas.

Wanda loved being the big cheese in the room, but around Uncle George, she acted like a sweet little flower. I knew better. I knew she was a hurricane waiting to devour some unsuspecting soul. Her continuous verbal ruminations, which were like sandpaper rubbing my skin raw, revolved around her, herself, and her some more. Even when she cooked and baked, it was more about "look what I did" than out of a desire to feed her children well. I watched her as she watched her soap opera. My insides burned with a flame fueled by anger and disgust. I hated who she was. I hated how she hurt others and me. I hated how she would never be like other moms and that she was mine. I compared her to my Aunt Betty and realized she was nothing more than a cruel beast. A bad person who called people names, and judged people, a racist who had sold her own daughters and bedded and married her daughter's first love. I started to burn with anger for the pain she inflicted on my older sisters, too, now IV drug users.

Wanda leaving me all alone in that motel was still fresh in my mind. The knowledge of how she left me with men she knew were sexually abusing me made me spin. Maybe she didn't know all the things they had done, or did she? Regardless, she had got her needs met through me and didn't care about what it had cost me. And now, I did not care about her either.

Rage would continue to fill me as I watched Wanda smack her Juicy Fruit. My body groaned when I reflected on what had happened to me and how she could just sit there in front of me watching TV, chewing her gum as if nothing had ever happened. I was not afraid to stay in our new home with my uncle. Wicked Wanda could leave our nest anytime now and never return. I welcomed the notion. She no longer needed me, and I thought I no longer needed her.

The Sparrow had never felt so cared for. Even so, she still lingered on tenterhooks. The Cloud of Black Hopelessness was replaced by a Raging Flame of Fire. She was fed with hatred and contempt for the one who had locked her inside a cage, raised a bow, and released arrows aimed straight at her heart. She was simultaneously being fed food that impregnated her with new dreams, and she devoured seeds full of hope, newness, and the ingredients it would take to create a different life for herself.

Chapter Fifteen
Goodbye Daddy

The rest of that year seemed like it flew by. I started school, made friends, and my hair even grew some. I worked with all my mental might to earn good marks. Unlike before, I eagerly wanted to get good grades. I became an honor student by the end of the first semester. My uncle and aunt would celebrate me by taking me out to a fancy dinner either with a new piece of jewelry and/or money. In addition, they didn't just celebrate my report cards, but any homework that came back with an "A." Aunt Betty even called her family in Venezuela to tell them I was on the honor roll when that happened. I loved to see them smile. The things that made them happy were so new and different. Wanda used to smile at me after we got through security at the prison when smuggling drugs inside. Drunk Gary would smile at me when he could tell he had said something mean enough to sting. My Dad would smile at me when I skipped a rock across the river, causing it to skip more than once. Shouting, "That's my girl," while throwing his arms up in the air; but grades, they never smiled nor frowned about those. Wanda would get annoyed when she had to stop for a minute to sign my report cards, let alone care about the marks I earned or the subjects I failed.

I wasn't popular at school, but I had a small tribe of friends. It felt so neat locking arms with other girls as we made our way down the halls. On the first day of school, Uncle George made Wanda sit in the passenger seat of the Cadillac as he drove me to my nearby bus stop. While I stood on the sidewalk waiting for my bus, they watched from the Cadillac. I felt so special. When I walked up those school bus steps, I did so with confidence knowing he was right there. My nerves attacked me once the bus pulled away—I told them everything would be okay...Yet, the further the bus got away from Uncle George, the stronger my struggle became.

The bus driver pulled up to my new school on that first day and pulled open the door. "Okay, I can do this," I told myself. After getting off the bus, I walked along a curb next to a sidewalk with that old feeling that eyes were looking at me, but instead of caving into my insecurities— I decided to look back into the eyes that were looking at me. Uncle George had told me that I never had to look down again. As I was walking through a school gate, I heard a horn honk just as I saw the back of the Cadillac pulling out of the parking lot. Uncle George looked at me as he slowly passed by on the road. He followed me all the way to school! I felt like a princess who had a King for an uncle.

But why had he followed me to school? I suddenly wondered. Were we still in danger? Was I in danger? Or did he simply want me to know he cared as I dreamed his reason to be. Then I thought about the time he told me how a group of kids picked on him when he was a young boy. Being small in stature and dirt poor with several young siblings tagging behind him made him an easy target for bullies. He told me they would wait until he was about halfway home near a wire fence before they would come out of the brush and ambush him. They would laugh at him and sing, "Georgie Porgie pudding and pie kissed the girls and made them cry." He told me how he often went home sporting a black eye and a fat lip until one day, Grandma Georgia took one of her stockings and filled it with stones. She tied a strong knot in both ends and told him to tuck it inside his jacket and to wait until they got up real close... then pull out the stocking... swirl it around, and "knock them right upside the head." Uncle George knew what it felt like to be mocked by peers, to be the unchosen one. He told me that after that day, those boys never bothered him again. In fact, he began to wait for them at the fence with his stocking full of stones, which Georgia said led to his fascination with weapons.

One day while sitting in my classroom, my name was called to the office. "That's weird. Why would I be called to the office? I silently questioned. I grabbed my backpack, hall pass and headed out... I had only been to the office where the principal set a few times. I spotted Wanda when I opened the door. "Oh, God, why is she here?" If I could have turned around and left without looking utterly disrespectful—I would have done so. Then I noticed she had been crying, but Wanda never cried. "Why was she here and why was she crying?"

"Jade," she sniffled. I looked at her with my new poker face. "Jade, it's your dad. Your dad killed himself." I stepped back, unable to speak. "What is she talking about, and why is she saying this?" I looked at the receptionist, and she looked like she was sharing my shock. Had my dad killed himself? Was my dad and his evil twin (AKA "Drunk Gary") dead? How could Wanda tell me this in front of all these people at my school? The oxygen was leaving the room, and so was I. Turning around swiftly, I aimed for the door. I ran down the hall and out the front doors. I didn't stop running. I wanted to get away from her. I needed to be alone. I ran until I hit a backstreet, then I slowed down as tears poured down my cheeks. I found a canal and sat next to it on a small dirt path, and sobbed until my soul ran dry. I thought of my dad. I couldn't see drunk Gary, no matter how hard I tried. All I could see was my dad lighting up one of his cigarettes, playing his guitar, singing Stairway to Heaven, and cracking coconuts on the front lawn. Was it true? Would I ever see my dad again? What happened to Tatiana? Suicide? Why?

Eventually, I got up and started walking home when Uncle George pulled alongside me. He rolled down the window, "Jade, get in" he commanded. I did as he requested. "Jade, your father was sick, sweetheart. Gary had a lot of problems from the war. I'm sure he loved you very much. This wasn't because of you, and there's nothing you or your mom could have done," he explained. My mom? Was he protecting her? What did she have to do with any of this? "I do not care about her," I coldly responded. Uncle George got that sniper look in his blue eyes, and in return, my best defiant look right back. "Jade, do you want to go to your father's funeral? Would you like to see your grandparents" he asked. I still felt like I couldn't breathe. How would I know what I wanted? A little pang perked up through my sadness when I thought about how I had been rude to my uncle. I looked at him and nodded my head yes.

A few weeks later, we were heading out of town to my dad's funeral. Aunt Betty came along even though she had never met my dad. I was grateful. We arrived at a cemetery. A cemetery full of parked cars. We headed into a side building. Hanging in front of the large room was a big picture of my dad wearing his army uniform and standing in front of the American Flag. I laid eyes on my grandma and grandpa and ran to them. Grandpa Pay opened his arms, and I ran into them, crying. I don't know why I cried so much or hurt so badly. My dad hadn't been very nice to me. He never even came to look for me. He laughed when I was scared, put me down into a crawl space when he was drunk, and kept me up late to purposefully torment me. But now all I could remember was the good times in between the bad. I looked at Grandma Drucilla, and she stared back at me with a catatonic gaze. She looked empty and unresponsive. On her lap sat a folded flag.

Not long after that moment, I watched my dad's body be lowered into the ground. I would never see him again. I would never have endless cups of hot cocoa with him at a 24-hour coffee shop while he smoked his cigarettes. I was trapped like a piece of fabric underneath "feed dogs" while a sewing machine brutally stitched the fact into me that I would never get to say goodbye to my dad—I would never see him again...Grandpa Pay pulled Wanda and me aside before we left the funeral. He held out a plastic bag with tape on it and handed it to me as he gently gestured forward and kissed my forehead. I hugged my grandpa again, noticing Uncle Alvin and Pete in the distance but decided to leave without saying goodbye to them.

When we got inside the car, Wanda asked me to hand her the bag, but I refused. But I did surprise myself when I realized I wanted her to look inside with me. I could already see his wallet with his chain on it, his zippo lighter, and his silver ring. I pulled out his wallet with a bunch of money inside it, but when we counted it, we learned there were a hundred and one-dollar bills folded up into a big wad. I reached for his ring and put it on my finger. It was way too big, but I kept it on. I didn't care. I would keep it forever. I then grabbed an envelope and opened it. Uncle George watched me intently through the rearview mirror as I read my dad's last words to me.

Dear Jade and Vicki, too,
It's your daddy here. I'm sorry I wasn't better to you girls. Mom has Alzheimer's, you know? Old Pay will be

forcing me to leave soon now that mom can't speak for me and you two never come around, so I'm playing out the card's life dealt me. I'm taking a lethal dose of my meds and going to sleep. Don't worry, it won't hurt, if you might worry. Be good for your mom and tell your other sisters' bye for me and your little brother too. Don't forget about your brother and sister I had with Nancy. The ones who got adopted by their foster parents. One day they might want to know about you girls and maybe even me.

Good night my little Sparrow and little Mouse. I'll see you both on the other side.

Love,

Daddy

Chapter Sixteen
Magdala

The death of my dad left me puzzled about so many things. I felt like I was in a world of wonder for the following two years while Wanda gained a new circle of friends. She began to invite neighbors over. I'd get home from school and walk into her sitting in the living room with a group of Christians having a bible study and playing music. Uncle George wasn't big on her involvement with the religious group but tolerated it.

Eventually, my uncle began to spend more time at his other house with Aunt Betty and less time with us. Lee moved into his room, and Uncle George popped in without notice. We never knew when he would show up. Wanda's leash was loosened. She had done what Uncle George asked of her and stayed away from drugs and alcohol. She still didn't have a job, but between the Social Security Survivor checks she received for Vicki and me and the financial assistance my uncle provided, we never went without.

I loved my uncle and aunt, but like a dance, I started to enjoy spending time in my own space while they enjoyed each other, and then smack, we would come back together again. However, slowly, the time in between our coming together expanded. Uncle George released the line connected to our lifesaver inch by inch, then foot by foot. We were drifting away into new waters.

I enjoyed spending time alone in my room, listening to music, reading, and journaling. The school became a happy place. I loved Junior High. The momentum which existed in 7th and 8th grade was right up my alley. Switching from class to class, having a different teacher in each one, and having my own locker felt like freedom. In a class I didn't care about, I would focus on the ones I did and put the minutes in my pockets until the bell would ring. Uncle George surprised me on my 12th birthday with a pet bird, a parakeet, inside a vintage-style iron cage. I named him "britches" because he looked like he was wearing pants. Britches learned to give me a kiss and wink at me; at least, I thought I trained him to do so.

I kept my dad's suicide letter inside a bible Wanda's new "spiritual friends" gave me. Wanda used the $101.dollar bills to take us out to dinner and bought me a silver chain to put my dad's ring on. She even placed it around my neck. She kept the zippo lighter and his wallet. That didn't bother me because she seemed genuinely upset.

I had never seen her cry like she cried after my dad died. I would lie on my bed and listen to her sobbing during the night. My parents had chatted occasionally, but they strongly hated each other through me. Wanda told me I was "mean and hateful" like my dad for as long as I could remember. Now, she cried like something catastrophic had happened to her. Once more, rendering her incapable of comforting me. I didn't get it.

I might have pushed her away if she had tried to comfort me during those first days of sadness and confusion, but moments would arise when I wanted her to try. But, yet again, I would receive no real comfort from the woman who had carried me inside her womb. The woman who told me how afraid she was that I would die like the little boy she had before me due to RH Factor. How she had managed to make it to a city 3- hours away during her last trimester to have injections put through her belly and into me to prevent my premature death. She bragged about how she was part of a clinical trial and how later scientists developed a medication to give to mothers who had RH Factor during and sometimes after the pregnancy in the arm versus the belly and no more than two injections. I found it interesting how a woman who endured the pain of needles going through her belly and into her fetus could care so little for that life once it was born.

Regardless of Wanda's efforts to destroy the lives she created, we found our way into a routine mimicking normalcy. Yet, lying within my new security blanket called "normal" were questions that troubled me. Like bolts of lightning and rumbles of thunder, they would suddenly appear, distracting me from the world around me.

Questions like, "why am I so sad my dad is dead? Then there was his letter, so casual? Would he have stayed alive if I went to see him more? I wanted to tell him that we didn't have a car and were miles away. How I wondered why he hadn't looked for me. How alone I had been too during those days at that motel. Is it possible, somehow, we could have saved each other? Did he loved me more than I knew?

I wondered if there was a heaven and a hell and if my Dad was still alive. Was God holding his hand, or was the Devil laughing at him? Maybe he was reincarnated into a cat or something. He hated cats. Or maybe Uncle George was correct, and he just simply ceased to exist.

Either way, his suicide was another stain on my soul and another secret to hide. Fortunately, no rumors I knew of spread around my school despite Wanda's lack of discretion. I told friends my dad had been in a bad accident. No one asked for details. However, the school counselor checked on me every now and then. I didn't want to talk about it, so I told her I was doing well to avoid her concerned looks. I didn't know her, and although she seemed nice, I didn't trust her enough to share my questions with her. I didn't share them with anyone. Let alone a stranger in a dress.

Wanda grew her hair to her waist and had a closet full of modest clothes by my eighth grade. She also started to go by the name Magdala. She regularly vanished to a house down the street for spiritual meetings and began taking Vicki and Lee with her. She invited me too, but I didn't want to go. She sometimes reminded me on her way out that Huff and Joker might be out of jail or have a hit on her so to keep the doors locked. She started saying things like, "Pride before a fall Jadey Pooh" when I rolled my eyes at her. She stopped flying off the handle and hitting me but would occasionally lose it and break a plate or slam her bedroom door. I braced myself when she got mad. Yet, I found myself wanting to make her mad. She was acting like someone else, but I still saw her. I saw the swastika and lighting bolt tattoos underneath the white ink.

"Jade, would you like to join us?" she sweetly asked while sitting at the kitchen table reading the bible and its companion book with her friend David. "No thanks. I have homework to do, Magdala" I exaggerated her new name as I slid by them. David was a tall and slender guy. He wore jeans and a dress shirt that looked the same every time I saw him. He had shoulder-length hair and wore glasses. He and Wanda read the Bible together and talked about God and some Prophet. He was quiet and seemed nice, but I felt uneasy around him.

He would say weird things like, "Jade, I see a dark cloud hovering over you. I believe it's unsettled energy in the spirit realm." Followed by the question, "can I pray for you?" He said God gave him the power to command spirits to leave and the power to shift spirit realms in atmospheres. He said Magdala had a "nurturing spirit and the gift of love." That's when I decided the guy was a nut. A picture of Grandma Georgia's nutcracker enlarged with David's head in between it flashed through my mind.

David said participating in school sports was "bad" and a "lure" by the evil one. When he learned I tried out for the eighth-grade basketball team, he read a scripture to me that said God commanded his people to be no part of the world. "Now, Jade, you don't want to go against the word of God, do you?" he asked.

My grandparents loved God; they never told me sports were bad. I joined the home team anyway and signed Wanda's name on the permission slip so David and Magdala wouldn't demonize me.

Wanda traded in her beloved TV shows for endless hours of the Prophet's sermons on tapes. The Prophet had a deep voice and talked a lot about the world ending. He said anyone who didn't know and follow the "truth" would be destroyed, which meant all but those who believed the same things as the Prophet, David, and Magdala. Wanda started to identify as a "child of God."

I felt like it was the Peckerwoods all over again, except these people looked and acted like clones and seemed high without drugs. Before long, Vicki and Lee started talking about the Prophet. Then, Wanda began to leave me with Uncle George and Aunt Betty while they traveled to large gatherings. She invited me, but I wanted to stay with my aunt and uncle.

Over time, it became apparent Wanda and David had more in common than a prophet and God. David sat us, kids, down one evening and told us the Prophet had told him that it was God's will for him to marry our mom. He asked us how we felt about that and explained how he would be the head of our household and our new father.

I did appreciate David's decency. He never touched Wanda sexually, and he didn't even hug her in front of me. It was so weird. I spent so much of my life watching Wanda engage in some kind of sexual activity. I recalled laying on a motel room floor next to Vicki and Lee while she had sex right above our heads. The song that was playing on the radio ran through my mind, "I've been waiting for a girl like you to come into my life..." I hated hearing that song.

David seemed to be the nicest guy Wanda had been with, but something was brewing underneath his cool demeanor. I grew to believe he had someone hiding inside him, like Wanda. I learned his problem with school sports was not limited to extracurricular activities. He had a huge problem with public schools and said there was a group of ladies in his church who taught children from home, but I loved school now. Now that I loved school and had friends, this nutcase and Magdala were trying to take it away from me. Aunt Betty said no one could take my education from me.

"No. I won't leave my school," I finally belted out. I won't leave my friends, my teachers. NO! "Now, Jade, it won't be tomorrow. I'll be sure you have plenty of time to say a proper goodbye," David calmly said. I looked Wanda straight into her eyes, "You can go, but I am not going anywhere. This is you trying to take me away from my friends. You are not a child of God! You are evil! You are Magdala the Witch!" I ran to my room and slammed the door. I screamed at the top of my lungs and beat my fists on the door. "I hate you; I hate you; I hate you," I shouted. "I will stay with my uncle and aunt. You guys leave," I continued.

Maybe I did have a demonic spirit hanging over me, and maybe it would send David running out the door with his sheepdog following behind him, or maybe David was seeing the Black Cloud of Hopelessness. Had it distracted me with the death of my dad? Had it come back to steal the joy I had found?

"Jade, your uncle, and aunt are leaving," I heard Wanda say from the other side of the door. Her words silenced my screams and shook me sober. What? I thought to myself. Is she lying? "Jade, I was gonna let George and Betty tell you, but here we are," she said. "They are going back overseas. Betty's dad is sick." I turned around and slid down my bedroom door. My heart cried, "Please, God, if you're real, please don't leave me alone with her. Not again. Not ever again."

The Sparrow raised her wing and looked down at the arrow lodged in her gut. She could see it, but she didn't have the ability to pull it out. She would need help.

Chapter Seventeen
Transitions

Wanda's words pierced my heart. My uncle would be leaving, and he told her first. My guardian angel would be thousands of miles away in a distant land. How could he leave me? I hadn't expected this to happen and completely missed it could. I got off the floor and walked over to Britches cage, "What are we going to do?" I asked him. I stared at him for the longest time taking in the fact that I would be left alone with Wanda again. I would be at her every whim and most likely have to move in with David and stay home from school with strange ladies. I would be like Britches. Caged once again.

"No!" I had to fight this. Ron turned David, and Wanda turned Magdala. What would they change my name to—Lucifer or Lucifina? I could run away, I thought. I would rather sleep under a bridge than live with her without my uncle's protection. I wondered if Grandma Georgia would let me live with her but then envisioned her hobbling throughout my school on her crutches, revealing her uneven heels, and handing out Bible tracts. Plus, she couldn't drive. I thought about Grandpa Pay but acknowledged he spent most days visiting Grandma Drucilla at the convalescent hospital, which would leave me alone with Uncle Pete.

Wanda acted differently and was nicer and more appropriate, but I still didn't trust her and believed she could revert to who she had been in a few seconds flat. I also had no idea what they did at David's house or their church, but I didn't feel all warm and fuzzy inside when they talked about God like I had when Grandma Georgia or Grandpa Pay had. Everything was becoming "bad" except for them.

    I grabbed hold of my courage and walked back into the living room. "I won't stay here if Uncle George leaves," I stated. "I want to go with him, or I will run away." David looked at me like he had just received a blow to the head. "Young lady. Do you know what the bible says about honoring your parents?" "Jade, you just need some time to adjust to these changes. I know you are upset that your uncle is leaving, but there is no reason for you to be so angry," he said. David had no idea what he was talking about. I had every right to be angry, every right to be upset, and every right to be afraid. "Do you know she sold drugs and even gave them to my older sisters when they were still teenagers?" I posed with a punch. Wanda looked like a deer in headlights. "Yes, Jade, yes, I do. Now the Lord forgives the transgressions of those who seek him and repent of their sins. Your mother is not the same person anymore. She is a brand-new creation. She is a strong tower now and one made of greatness that's why God gave her the name Magdala." "Would you like to repent, Jade, for dishonoring your mother?" "God will forgive the sins of those who turn away from their wicked ways," he went on. Just then, I realized he reminded me of a drug-free, God-fearing Nick Mills. Instead of shoving rags down my throat, this guy was going to use bible verses to suffocate me. "I told ya, David. See what I mean? Jade's always been this way. She came out of me hollering," Wanda whispered. "I can hear you," I screamed. "I want to talk to my uncle now," I demanded.

My uncle walked through the door before the hour was up. When I looked into his blue eyes, I knew it was true. No words were needed. I clenched my jaw together and tried to keep the lump in my throat from swelling, but I couldn't. I let out a gasp and fell to my knees, sobbing. My soul groaned in pain. Knowing he was leaving hurt so much more than when my Dad died. I would miss Aunt Betty too.

"Jade, get up," my uncle said as he gestured for me to stand up. He walked me into my room, and together we sat on Vicki's bed. He took his right hand and placed two fingers in front of his eye, "look into my eyes, Jade." I lifted my head, trying to act strong. I held his gaze. "You and I are cut from the same cloth. You are stronger than you know. You are tough as nails Jade, and unlike my sister, you are smart. This world is a dog-eat-dog place. You need to decide what you want and how you want to live your life and do what you need to do to get there. Jade, look at me," he said again. Realizing I was looking at my feet, I lifted my head again. "Don't ever quit on yourself," he commanded with his sniper eyes. He went on to explain that Wanda was in a better position in life now and how they needed to return to Saudi Arabia to care for Betty's father and her family's company.

I knew my uncle and aunt had sacrificed a lot to help us, and I could feel my uncle's sincerity. I nodded my head with eyes that said I understood.

"George, if she really doesn't want to live with me, maybe she can go to Sandy's, June's oldest daughter. She took in little Johnny," Wanda offered as she appeared in the doorway. I had met Sandy a few times, but I didn't really know her. She seemed nice, had a husband named Terri, and a few sons. Sandy was my first cousin and had a reputation for taking in strays. I knew she lived far away by a forest filled with Redwood trees, and there was an Ocean shore just a few blocks away from her house. I conjured up a vague memory I had of Wanda taking us there to visit. Aunt Junie and my other cousins were there too. I remembered the long drive more than anything else. It was far away. Yes, I want to be far away from Wanda. I will go there if she will have me, I thought to myself. A spark of hope lit inside me.

Uncle George and Aunt Betty had to leave just shy of my 8th-grade graduation but celebrated with me prior. They took me to a fancy seafood restaurant and gave me a beautiful necklace. It had a glass pendant that was filled with flakes of gold they said came from Saudi Arabia. They told me to wear the necklace and keep it close to my heart as a reminder of how much they loved me. Now I wore two necklaces— both representations of people who once were and of people who would be no more.

Wanda planned an 8th-grade graduation party for me as she and David made wedding plans. Everything would be shifting that June. I would turn 14 years old. The beautiful house we had been living in would no longer be ours. Wanda, Vicki, and Lee would be moving in with David, and I would be moving to the far northern coast of California. Another change was happening. My body had started to develop. I also grew several inches. Wanda had been hell-bent that I would be "short and fat" like my Grandma Drucilla, but now I loomed over her by 5 inches. Something about that made my heart happy. I also caught up to her in jean size. Wanda still shopped in the juniors' section as she was on the petite side and would still say things like, "I'm not shopping over there in the old ladies' section" when referencing the women's department. I also noticed boys at school were looking at me differently. One popular boy even asked me if I was "new at school" for the first time, I could say, "no, I've been here since the start of 7th grade," as I turned and walked away. I did look different. My breasts grew so fast that I got stretch marks, and as painful as it was, I went shopping with Wanda to buy a bra. I didn't like it when she talked about my developing body. Her words sent chills up my spine and grossed me out. I wasn't sure how to feel regarding the changes I was physically experiencing. Part of me was glad that I was starting to look more like the other girls instead of like a boy. Part of me liked the new attention and looks I was getting. Then part of me was utterly embarrassed. It was as if I was walking through my junior high school halls with two left feet.

The day came when I said goodbye to my human savior and his high-class wife. I felt like part of my heart was packed in their cargo and left on that plane with them. I loved them and would be forever grateful for what they had done. I had dreamed I would see their faces in the audience as I received my 8th-grade diploma, but instead, I saw David and Magdala. They didn't even bring Vicki and Lee because they had already been placed in home school, and they didn't want them to be influenced by the crowd of worldly people.

Afterward, we had a small gathering with Wanda's new friends. A lady from their church made me a gorgeous cake, and David invited a few kids my age to attend. They were nice and acted overly enthusiastic about meeting me. I noticed right away that the boys my age were dressed just like David. They acted differently than my friends at school. They carried a flare of innocence. I could see they were, indeed, no part of the world I knew.

David and Magdala were married on June 22, 1989, by the Prophet inside a beautiful white building called "Church." Vicki and Lee walked down the aisle, arm in arm, looking delicately sweet in their wedding attire. I was surprised to see how many ladies walked down the aisle before Wanda. All the men were already standing by David. As the women approached the Prophet, they would stop momentarily until he nodded at each one of them before they took their place on the other side of his pulpit. Then Magdala appeared wearing white from head to toe. I couldn't help but admit to myself she looked stunning. She beamed like the sun on a garden-fresh spring day. She walked towards the Prophet like she was walking towards God himself, like a chosen virgin going to the altar. Their ceremony was long. I started to itch to get out of there, but I would have to endure hours with these people. Sandy and Teri would not be arriving until the following day. We stayed with David's mother the night of their wedding. She was a nice woman whose hair was held high by a tight gray bun. She moved around a lot, like she had one task after another to complete until it was time to go to bed.

The following day I loaded my suitcase into the back of Sandy and Terri's pickup truck. I said goodbye to Vicki, Lee, and my little friend Britches and set forth to begin my new life with my cousins on the coast of California.

God heard the Sparrow's heart cries and found someone to help her. She was flying to a new place, to a new home, with new people.

Chapter Eighteen
Passing Through

Sitting in the front seat of Sandy and Terri's pickup truck with them felt odd. I knew my cousin, Sandy, but I didn't. A familiar stranger. They arrived around 1:00 am, stayed at a motel, and here they were just hours later, heading home with a new addition in tow. They were friendly, and both wore smiles. They looked like one of those couples whose features molded together over time. I had heard they married when Sandy was 16 years old. Teri was older, but I didn't know how much.

They were my Taxi to get far away from Wanda, but I didn't feel as relieved as I thought I would. I was nervous. I wondered if I had made a mistake before we made it out of town. I was leaving everything I knew, including Vicki and Lee, once again. I put a smile on my face trying to match theirs, but inside I was filled with fear. I didn't want to be afraid. I wanted to feel as strong as I was determined to let Wanda know I would rather live with mere strangers than be left alone with her again. I bravely went through the proper motions as I had done so many times before, but a small voice inside of me screamed out in despair. I found myself feeling as if I were alone in the world once again. Two adults sat next to me, happy to take me home, traveled for hours to pick me up, and even made space for me in their home, but I felt displaced. The drive sparked the emotions I had when the lady from child protective services drove me to Kris and Sophia's house. However, I had made the choice this time.

Sandy and Terri asked me if I owned a windbreaker for the coastal weather. When I told them I didn't, they stopped as we drove through one of the cities. They ended up buying me more than just a windbreaker and seemed happy to lavish me with new clothes. They also bought items for their two sons, Little Johnny, and some for my other cousin, who I learned was staying with them. Her name was Casandra. She was 15 years old and had a child. She was the daughter of one of my aunts from Georgia. An Aunt who strongly disapproved of Casandra getting pregnant before marriage. I started doing math in my mind and made up about eight of us who would live together. Four cores and four strays.

I considered the new clothes to be a gesture of kindness. I could tell Sandy and Teri was trying to make me comfortable. I complied even though my heart was not in it and hid my heart posture with "thank you's" and smiles. The drive North was as long as I recalled. Daylight eventually faded into darkness, leading to the silence inside the truck. My cousin slept with her head resting on her husband's shoulder as I sat wide awake next to her. I was sleepy, too; however, my adrenaline was turned on and turned up like I had received a shot of epinephrine. I sat against the passenger, door-heart racing—stiffened with silence. When suddenly, I felt something tap my knee. I set up taller as rigamortus consumed my limbs. I felt it again, only this time warmth from someone's hand covered my knee. I looked down to see Teri's arm stretched around the front of my cousin while his hand cradled my kneecap. A thought did not pass through my mind before I reached down and grabbed his hand, and threw it away from me. Supercharged, I bent around my cousin and shot fiery darts out of my eyes at him. Cognizant, I was in the proximity of another pervert, I was determined he would not touch me again.

The rest of the drive was nearly intolerable. I was stuck in a puddle of turmoil as I had stepped into quicksand. I sank into my seat, unable to climb out of the pickup truck or my decision. Still, before we arrived, I decided I would not take any future attempts by Teri lying down. I would fight him with all I had if he tried to touch me again. He would not have me, nor would he touch me. No one would EVER touch me again without my permission. I would raise alarms and die fighting before anyone would trespass on my body again.

Eventually, we ran into the Northern California coastal breeze carrying the aroma of sea salt and seaweed. Sandy woke up, which eased the tension in the cab tremendously. We pulled into the little town and up to my new home. It was the typical seaside home you'd expect to see in a small coastal town. It was dark, but I could see succulents lacing a little white picket fence in the front yard. The house was shell pink with blue trim, and a life buoy hung near the front door. The house was longer than wide and looked like it was slightly tilted. Tilted or not, I was happy to get out of the truck.

Sandy cheerfully led me into a slightly dimmed hallway. The house was quiet, and everyone was sleeping. I would have to wait until morning to meet my relatives and be reunited with Little Johnny. My sweet cousin showed me and my suitcase into a bedroom that had 6-foot-tall bookshelves lined down in the middle. The bookshelves were rotated, exposing shelves on one side, then the back of a bookcase, then another set of shelves. I saw a twin bed with someone sleeping in it on one side before Sandy told me it was Little Johnny. There were two nightlights. One on his side and one on mine. I realized I would be sharing a room with my nephew, which decreased some of my concerns about Teri coming into the room while I slept. I went to the bathroom and locked the door behind me before changing into my PJ's. Then I made my way back into my and Little Johnny's room and into my twin bed.

The following morning, I woke to the sound of chatter and laughter. It was hard for me to handle the fact that only a few days had passed since I woke up in my beautiful room with Britches chirping nearby. Now I was far away from there, far away from that day. Everything seemed surreal to me. While at our home with Uncle George, things had changed radically around me, like Wanda turned Magdala, for example, but I had slept in the same bed every night and felt safe doing so for nearly three years. I had finally been moving through life with the same group of kids at school, and now here I was, once again adrift. I would have to build new relationships with the people I lived with, possibly contend with sexual advances by Teri, and explain to people why I lived with my cousins instead of a mom and dad. The weight of it was trying to cripple me. I had to hold the boulder at bay. I am tough as nails, like Uncle George said. I can do this. I have no other options. I got up and found some clothes before slowly but surely making my way through the crowd and into the bathroom to change.

"Jade, Jade" yelled Little Johnny. "Hey, buddy, how are you?" I asked as Johnny ran to me. He had grown several feet, and his little face ballooned. His red hair looked like fire, and he had cute little freckles which made a path across his nose. He certainly didn't look like Big Johnny or my sister, but he was very cute. I had always felt bad for him. For some reason, I bore a sadness and a sense of guilt for what my mother had done. She had stolen his father away from his mother. His grandma married his father, making Lee his younger uncle and half-brother. Making me not only his aunt but, for a while, his stepsister. Weird how Little Johnny and I landed here together, I pondered.

"Hi Jade, I'm Casandra," said my doll faced cousin. "It's like so neat you're here. I've been excited to meet you. Do you know the ocean is super close? I hope we can, like, go lay out on the beach or do something like that together," she said as she twirled her hair. She seemed nice and appeared to favor the word "like." Then there was Toby and James. They were about as opposite as the opposite could be. Toby was stalky with dark hair and eyes—stealthy. James was skinny with blue eyes and blonde hair—skittish. I glanced at Sandy and then quickly at Teri, who smiled from ear to ear. What a weirdo! I thought as I saw his face morph into a Cheshire cat.

"Get some sleep?" Sandy asked. "Ya, I slept good," I replied with a smile. "Well, go have some cereal before we head to the park." The park? "I'll show you where it's at, Jade" Little Johnny grabbed my hand and led me into the kitchen. It didn't take long for me to realize how happy he was that I was there. He and his four siblings had been shuffled around throughout our family because my sister was buried deep within a dark world of addiction. Too sick, too wounded to care for her own. Somehow, I had escaped that horrible affliction and was preparing to head out on a joyous adventure with my cousins. Guilt ate away at my heart when I thought about it.

Everyone except Terri loaded into Sandy's minivan before noon and headed to the park. My eyes widened as we approached the Jedediah Smith forest entrance. It was daylight now, and I could see the beauty that surrounded me. There were towering redwood trees that appeared to be reaching for the heavens. I inhaled the earth as I stepped onto a narrow path behind my cousins and Little Johnny. Pine needles, dirt, and bark filled my nostrils with their freshness.

I was consumed by the landscape—an emerald city. Trees overshadowed me instead of buildings. Large ferns sprang up from all four corners. Fallen trees were covered with moss turning them into mystic madness. I was intrigued by every aspect of this whimsical world. I could hear water rushing somewhere in the distance, but waves of fog shielded my sight. I continuously laid my eyes on something unfamiliar and beautiful as I made my way through the fallen clouds. The "park" was magical. I was in love.

"You know parts of Star Wars were filmed here," Sandy said as she bounced on a patch of dead pine needles. I can see why, I said to myself. We spent that day running throughout the magical forest, walking on fallen trees, and picnicking underneath the blue sky. My dry skin from the desert sucked up the moisture in the air, and I felt incredible. Maybe this was a good decision after all. The evening was filled with cooking and eating, followed by a movie. We all sat around and watched a film together which was kind of cool. I still felt like a guest inside a stranger's home, but I was settling in. I did my best to ignore Teri's presence altogether by not looking in his direction when he spoke and by not engaging in any conversations that he was a part of. At night, Little Johnny and I would lie in our beds and speak to each other over the bookshelves that separated us.

"Jade, have you seen my mom?" Little Johnny asked. "Not in a long time Johnny" I replied. Fortunately, that was the truth of the matter. And the delivery of that truth hurt my heart. "Hey, Johnny." "Yeah?" "Your mom loves you. She is just really sick. It is not your fault, buddy. I promise you. It is not your fault." "Do you think I'll get to see her again and see my brothers and sisters?" he asked. "Yes, Johnny. You will. I don't know when, but the day will come when you will get to see them again. One day you'll be able to drive and go wherever you want to go and see whoever you want to see. I promise. That day will come." I assured him. And it will come for me, I reassured myself. I wanted to hold him and tell him everything would be okay, but I knew to comfort him too much would be a mistake. I knew we were crossing paths and that I would not be able to carry him along on my journey. "Goodnight, Johnny. I love you, and your mommy loves you too," I whispered. "Goodnight, Jade, love you too," Little Johnny whispered back.

Only a few days passed before Casandra, Little Johnny, and I headed down to the beach. I had to shake my feet repeatedly on the way to kick sand out of my sandals. The sidewalks were covered with pebbles and sand. Before I could see the ocean, it made its enormous body known by the sounds of its raging waves and the mist of water it sent to dampen my face. Again, exhilaration toppled me. The smells, the feels, the fresh air...What is this? I asked myself. My body and mind became absent of anything bad or worrisome when I entered into the realm of the great vast sea and through the gates of the magical emerald city. I had never experienced something so powerful, something that was able to wash away my internal debris when I stepped inside its kingdom.

The Sparrow was nestled inside Mother Nature's bosom. The thumping of her heartbeat silenced all that ailed the maturing Sparrow. The Sparrow fell in love with something new but understood she was just flying through.

Chapter Nineteen
Rebound

Days rolled into nights, and nights rolled into weeks. I slept most nights with a window cracked above my bed so that the airy coastal breeze could drizzle through. I spent many nights having late-night conversations with Little Johnny over our bookshelves. I loved him with my words as much as I could while keeping the walls around my heart secure.

One day while Sandy and Teri were out, Casandra asked me if I wanted a Tequila Sunrise. I didn't know what that was, but by her expression, I knew it was something taboo. "Come on, it is like the best drink ever," she declared while holding up a bottle of Tequila. "But Teri works at the prison. Isn't that dangerous to do?" I questioned. I already didn't especially care for the guy. I wasn't about to give him ammo to fire. Plus, I didn't want to be the type of person who fell into wells of liquor. I hated drugs and alcohol. I hated what they had done to me, to my family. A family that could have been different if its veins were not contaminated by poisons.

"No, I think I'll pass," I said. "Oh, jade, don't be such a prude. Fine, I'll only put like a little tiny bit in yours. It will be mostly orange juice. I promise, come on, don't be such a chicken," Casandra went on. I didn't want to get caught by her lures, but I did fill a hook and then a tug. I'm not like my mom or dad. I am different. Alcohol won't make me do the things they did or act the way they acted, I thought to myself. "Okay, just one," I said. Casandra smiled as she did a little dance while making our drinks. "I knew you weren't a total dud, Jade."

Casandra then led me to her and her daughter's room, where she pulled out a ton of swimsuits. "Let's lay out on top of the roof. Brittney's sleeping and I can like hear her cry if she wakes up, and it will be like so much fun to lay out and drink together," Casandra continued. Everything about the encounter felt cringe-worthy, but despite my discomfort, I went along. Only I insisted on wearing a long T-Shirt over the two-piece swimsuit she loaned to me. Together we climbed to the top of the roof and laid on large towels. I could tell this was something she had done before. The road was carved.

At first, the drink tasted like I was swallowing poison, but as it went down, the taste of chemicals faded into the sweetness of orange juice and grenadine. My head felt a little fuzzy, and like the effects of the landscape, the glass I held in my hand contained a magical potion that was able to silence my trepidations. I'm not sure how many more I had before I had stripped my T-Shirt off and was dancing in Casandra's slim bikini on the rooftop. I even belted out a few tunes while forgetting what lay beneath the eves.

"Jade, are you okay?" Cassandra questioned as my head began to spin. I nearly fell over before bending to a sitting position. I threw my body back onto the roof, allowing the sun to penetrate my skin, but I was dizzy and was going to be sick. I sat up and hurled all over the shingles next to my towel and myself. Through a haze, I watched my vomit trickle down the side of the roof and drip onto a concrete walkway in the backyard.

"Oh my god, Jade. You like drank like way too much. We need to get down and, like, get you into bed before Sandy and Teri get home" Casandra begins to panic. "I don't care, who cares? I'm fine." Stammering, I took my hand and pushed at the air in the direction of Casandra as if to say, "bug off." My head was spinning, and I felt like I was going to hurl again, and then I did.

An overwhelming fishy smell hit my nose and woke me from a dead sleep. It was dark, and I was in my bed. How did I get here? I struggled to recall making my way down the rooftop and into my room as I pulled my blanket up to my face, covering my nose, but the smell coming from the kitchen was inescapable. I needed to go to the bathroom, but I didn't want to walk through the living room to get there. Remorse and embarrassment shackled me to my bed. Oh no, I cringed when I remembered myself awkwardly dancing and singing on the rooftop. Oh god, what a fool, what did I do? Had Casandra cleaned up my vomit? Did Teri and Sandy know? I peeked underneath my covers to discover I was still wearing Casandra's bikini and nothing else. Oh my god, kill me now. I felt sick. For the first time, I experienced the blackness I was told about. The periods of time which should be considered "excusable" because alcohol was involved. However, I didn't feel like this was okay. I felt bad and humiliated. I felt like I had cheated myself. Is that how my mom and dad felt? I wondered. At the same time, I reflected on how warm and fuzzy the drinks made me feel. How, for a while, I was brave enough to show skin, dance, and even sing. I hadn't danced since I was a little girl spinning around in the living room at my grandparent's house. Additionally, I could not carry a tune to save my life. But was it worth it? I was too embarrassed to get out of bed wearing the bikini, too afraid someone would see me. I felt sick and ended up having to hold my pee for hours. Plus, I didn't like the blackness. The not remembering. What else happened? I fretted with fear and the frustration of not being able to remember getting down from the roof and walking into the house.

The following morning, I grappled with remnants of embarrassment as I made my way into the kitchen. Sandy took the boys' school clothes shopping and had to tidy up enrollment at their elementary school. She planned to take me on a tour of what would be my new high school later that week. I made myself a bowl of Wheat O's and sat down at the table when Teri walked in. He was wearing his uniform. He looked different when he was wearing his prison gear— intimidating. The sensation of uneasiness around law enforcement was engraved into my bones. I've done nothing wrong; I've done nothing wrong, I would tell myself when a cop pulled behind us or when I passed a security guard inside a mall, but this time I had done something wrong. As Teri nodded his head at me, I flashed back to a moment when I was standing in front of security at San Quentin state prison, praying for the hidden drugs on the conveyor belt to remain concealed.

"Cassi, come here," Teri called from the sink. Casandra came into the kitchen, bouncing little Brittney on her hip. "Ya, Teri?" she asked. Teri reached his hand above the sink and pulled out the bottle of tequila. Looking at her, he tapped the bottle's side while his Cheshire Cat smirk ran across his face. "Now, Cassi, you know the rules don't you." He said seductively with a tilt of his head. "No drinking alone, ladies," he said as he put the bottle away. "Teri, you are so funny. You totally got me." Casandra replied while flipping her head back and throwing a cutesy smile his way. On his way out, Teri bumped into my chair, purposefully revealing handcuffs hanging from his gun belt. I looked up at Casandra with a look of disgust, not fully comprehending what had just transpired but sensing a familiar eeriness.

We were nearing fall as summer was ending when I witnessed the weirdness that existed between Teri and Casandra. I had already lost all respect for Teri during our first encounter when he touched my knee, but over time white elephants multiplied in every room of that shell pink house, cementing my skepticism. When one day, we were all gathered in the living room to hear the news that Teri had been transferred to a lower security prison, which appeared to be something they had been hoping for. A move to a large city would take place before me and the boys started school. Soon afterward, Casandra announced she and Brittney would be moving in with one of her older sisters. The few things I liked about living with them were having the ocean nearby, Little Johnny, and even Casandra. My doll-faced cousin stood between me and my fears concerning Teri. Two of the three would be gone. I lay awake in bed, unable to sleep for hours after that news. Boxes were brought home within a few days, and packing started. I hadn't spoken to Wanda since I arrived there, but I suddenly felt desperate to hear her voice. I still felt displaced, and at least with Wanda, I didn't feel like a stranger, a guest. Being with them revealed an invisible bond between Wanda and me that I hadn't wanted to acknowledge. One that just was. A bond of comfort even in the discomfort. A bond that shouted home even when my bed was a motel room floor. A bond that was simply an attachment to a woman I had always known.

 I would have to decide between a new life in a big city with Teri or a new life with Wanda and David and their religion. Neither option made my heart sing, but they were the two I had. I contemplated what it would feel like to leave Little Johnny and knew it would be horrible. In some ways, it would be even more painful than leaving Vicki and Lee. I considered Wanda and David's religion and what that would involve. I knew there would be no high school, no prom.

Then there was the voice of resentment which still lived inside me towards Wanda. How would I navigate that with her and a new stepfather? I questioned if paranoia from my past was altering my current reality with regard to Teri, but ultimately decided to trust my gut. I had to get out before things escalated. I would not be at this prison guard's disposal, nor would I want to hurt Sandy by telling her about her husband's advancement or my suspicions. At least David was a Christian man. Driven by the panic of the unknown, I called the known.

"Hi, mom, it's me, Jade. I want to come home..." I said. "We'll be leaven to get ya in the morning...," she said.

The Sparrow would be migrating south for the winter with her mother. Returning to a nest, she had been desperate to flee. She hoped her new home, her redeemed mother, would provide the warmth and security she needed.

Chapter Twenty
Farmland

Leaving my coastal clan was bittersweet. I exchanged a happy embrace with Lee for a sad goodbye with Little Johnny. The atmosphere inside the living room became thick with tension when Wanda walked through the door after that summer's passing. I was about an inch taller and had filled out physically since our last encounter at her wedding. I caught her observations of my mature feminine physique as her eyes darted my way. Our reunion revealed two people still chaffed by each other's presence. Two people carrying suitcases full of skeletons inside their minds. Nevertheless, two people who were bound by a blood bond. No big smiles and no sentiments were exchanged. The slim smiles directed at each other were as inconsistent as our fleeting eye contact, but she had come. The orphan inside me clung to the fact that I called, and she responded. I thought she might have done so for the monthly check she would receive for me, but I presumed that paycheck was extra income for Sandy too. Only I believed Sandy's heart was in the business of fostering relatives for more reasons than money.

I felt like I was standing close to a live wire carrying high-voltage anxiety when I stood near Wanda. One that would have zapped away the wall of ice which had separated my mom from me. I realized that the wall had dissolved, and in its place stood a concrete dam filled with floating scars.

However, like pressure released from a tire's valve causing it to lose air was the release I felt as I walked out of that shell pink house, down the little concrete path, past the white picket fence laced with succulents, and into the passenger's seat of Wanda's new bronze sedan.

"Jade, you get to meet Duke, Esther, and Noah. Britches will be happy too!" My little brother excitedly exclaimed from the backseat. "I can't wait, Lee. Who are they?" I asked. "Duke is our dog, he's real real big, he jumps a lot, but he doesn't bite. So don't be scared. Esther is a girl goat, and Noah is a boy goat. They were born together on the farm with other goats, but we could only have two. They still have horns. Dad says they keep them cooler in summer, and they can fight other animals with them, but they won't hurt you, Jade. I promise!" Lee enthusiastically continued. It was so good hearing the sweet innocence his voice carried and how I loved him. He and Vicki had blossomed as I had over the summer. They were still very thin and delicate in nature with large curious eyes, but I noticed Vicki seemed more reserved. Her princess-like demeanor seemed to have turned a bit icy during my absence.

Quiet, reserved, legs crossed. She sat with a posture equivalent to a well-made statue as she read her bible in the backseat. She certainly wasn't as happy to see me as Lee, but the depth of our distance had been descending since our stay at the cockroach motel. Her focus on efforts for Wanda's love meant she had to choose her side over mine to win her approval. My friendship with Kaira and Darsh had also saddened her, causing her to feel excluded. So, her indifferent attitude wasn't a big surprise. I briefly reflected on how Lee had referred to David as "Dad." It was weird to hear David's new title out loud. However, that, too, did not come as a surprise.

That evening we stopped and ate together at a restaurant before heading to a motel to rest for the night. Wanda was quiet from the moment we left Sandy's until our eyes closed. It was an uneasy silence, but more biting would have been the force of unwanted words. I could see a change in her, but I wondered if any part of her was sorry for what she had done to my older sisters and me. I wondered why there had always been so much distance between us and if she had truly turned into a good mom. Could we ever be friends like some moms and daughters? Would we ever sit on the bow of a boat together while laughing and tilting our hats to the wind, or would our potential to love each other remain lost at sea indefinitely?

The following day we left before the morning's dew evaporated. As we continued our way south, Wanda finally started a conversation with me, "You have your own room down at the house." David put a wall up in an office he had. He sheet rocked it and painted it for you." She reported. "He's a good man. I don't need you causing any trouble for me." She closed. I clenched my jaw and dug my fingernails into the palm of my hand as I looked out the passenger window. Old Queen Lunacy made her presence known before we hit the farming community we were headed to. At least she isn't on drugs or alcohol, I told myself, begrudgingly irritated by her internal paranoid narrative. It was a narrative that told her that my intent from birth was to harm her in some way.

"Yay! We're here," shouted Lee. "Thank goodness," said Vicki. To their credit, it had been a long drive. Wanda made what could have comfortably been broken into a 4–5-day drive in 3 days. I spotted a gas station far off the interstate as a giant tumbleweed whirled across the freeway, twirling onto the reddened landscape before dancing between cactus's riddled with prickly pears ready to eat.

We came to a dirt road secured by a large gate. "Keep Out" and "Private Property" signs covered the powerlines leading to it. The security gate also held signs reading "Trespassing Prohibited" and "Surveillance Notice." Lee jumped out and opened the gate. He had turned into a little man. I mulled over how much he and everyone else had seemed to change. I was about to meet David as a Stepfather and live with him. I would be living with Wanda and their community of friends. I breathed deeply as if I was about to step on a stage in front of a thousand people as we entered through the big metal gate. My left foot wiggled wildly like it had a mind of its own. We passed a white modular home, then another, then another.

"Mom, are these all the same?" I asked. "No. These are members who haven't built homes on the property. Most of us have houses down yonder." Modular homes lined the dirt road on both sides. Livestock lived inside fenced closures, but a few goats and several chickens roamed about freely.

"You have to go real real slow, Jade. Look, Jade, that's where Ester and Noah were born, Lee said as he pointed to a large red barn with a massive windmill spinning near it. Tall cornstalks filled what could have been a football field. That I liked. It was beautiful. I imagined running through the cornfield and getting lost in its organic maze. Few people walked about. However, the people I saw looked, nodded, and then turned away. With the windows down, I could hear the bleating of goats and dogs barking in the distance, but other than the sounds of animals, the community seemed quiet. At least for the first several hundred acres. There was something peaceful about the ambiance of the place.

We eventually drove past an area free of modules and houses. Just barren land lived in those spaces. There was a pond. It was huge. I could see ducks floating on the water. I could also see myself jumping into that pond in the future. I couldn't help smiling as I envisioned sitting on the bank with my toes in the water. To my right, I notice the frame of a new house surrounded by wood scaffolding and young men. Some even looked my age. They were speckled about while some carried hammers, beams and wore toolbelts like men for hire. However, Wanda explained they were all "brothers" who lived in the community and had been assigned to build that home. She told me they built the homes as a service to God, "not for money like people in the world."

They nodded politely as we passed. One even caught my eye. He was medium built and had dark shoulder length hair. He looked like he was Hispanic or Indian. His brown eyes connected with mine for a moment. A fixed gaze powerful enough to slow down time and burn his image into my brain was exchanged between us. His brown skin was a vision of perfection in the sun. He was a vision of perfection. He looked about 17 or maybe a few years older. I didn't have the best gauge for age, but I knew he couldn't have been too old.

"How long is this road?" I asked Wanda. "We got about 400 acres. Road's bout an eight-minute drive. It felt like we had been driving longer than that, but I guessed it was the slowness of our speed and the length of the dirt road leading to the entry gate. Eventually, on the other side of the pond, scattered houses became visible like dots on dice leading to a tall steepled building. The large white church sat centrally and at the lowest point on the property. In front of it, the dirt road looped around to the other side of the pond, eventually reconnecting with the main narrow dirt road you drove in on. It appeared there was one way in and one way out—through the large metal gate and barbed wire fence that surrounded it.

We pulled up to "our" house. Here I was again, about to meet my new bedroom. I saw David walk out of the front door and towards the car before I heard him ask, "Hello, young lady. How are you? "Hot and tired," I replied with a soft giggle. "Well, let me get your things," David offered as Lee ran up and threw his arms around him. "Hey, little man. It's good to see you." Kneeling down to Lee's eye level, he asked, "Did you take care of your mom and sisters like I asked you to?" Lee shook his head up and down. David patted the top of his head and said, "Good job, buddy," as he continued his walk to the trunk, "Remember, the bible says a man has a greater responsibility than a woman. One day you will be the head of your household Lee. You have been given the gift of being a man by God. Just don't forget God's law on that arrangement." I almost felt like he was talking to the wind at a certain point. I was listening because I was listening to every sound in my new environment, but Lee was standing there with a dazed look. I knew what stood behind that blank stare. He was thinking, "Hurry up, so I can go play with the goats." I laughed to myself as I observed Lee stand in obedience as his mind transported to where he would be as soon as David shut up.

I had just arrived, and David had already started his preaching, but he did seem nice. Especially compared to other men who had been in Wanda's life and mine. The land was clean, and the house was comfortable. It was brick red and had a chimney poking out of the tin roof. On the inside the house was wood from floor to ceiling. I had imagined crosses hanging everywhere, but I didn't see any. The inside of the house was a mixture of Western décor and bleakness. As though it was decorated to send the feel of coziness but felt like one of those mid-grade motel suites you might rent in a remote country mountain community.

My room had a simple twin-size bed covered with what looked like a handmade quilt. There was a desk with a lamp on it. I also saw an oversized hourglass which I thought was kind of cool, and different—in the center sat a bible with a notepad next to it. There was a slim wood dresser that appeared to have been handcrafted. All in all, the room felt peaceful.

While I was taking it all in, David appeared, standing in the doorframe. He told me to make myself at home and shared with me that there would be a community movie night at the hall the following evening. I thanked him politely for the room and inquired about the hourglass. He replied, "Well, Jade, here in this household, we have times of study and private fellowship with God. That there is an hourglass lasting exactly that, an hour. Every day, you pick the time, I will expect you to read your bible, pray, and write down the scriptures you read and what they mean to you. Then we will meet in a family discussion to make sure your understanding is in proper alignment with the word of God and the Prophet's revelations. Jade, we have rules here, which I understand might be difficult for you, but the Prophet said

God has given me the grace to help you understand what God expects from a young lady. Please, understand everyone here in this community is your family. You are surrounded by people who love you and look forward to meeting you. I know you have been hurt, but God wants to take all that old pain away from you and replace it with love." He nodded like every other stranger I had seen in the "community." He smiled, tapped his hand on the doorframe, turned, and walked away.

I got up and closed my bedroom door and was extremely relieved to find it locked from the inside. Hearing about God was not new for me. Grandma Georgia and Drucilla and Grandpa Pay had all spoken to me about it. So, David's words seemed to slow down the hamster wheel spinning inside my mind, even though I found him overzealous and on the nutty side. I lay on what was my new bed and stared at the knotty pine ceiling. I wondered if the guy I saw with the beautiful brown skin would be at this community movie night, David mentioned. When I closed my eyes, I saw his face. When I envisioned his face, my body tingled all over. My desire to see him again was exhilarating. I had never liked a boy before and had sworn to myself I would never give myself to a man sexually unless I knew he loved me enough to marry me if I ever would at all. I was still only 14, but I knew what sex was, and it had always been a painful and traumatic experience for me. Yet, the tingling and giddiness inside me over road my painful memories of being hurt by men and having to listen to and sometimes see Wanda have sex. One gaze from this carpenter boy starved the venomous bite of those memories and stomped their stinging burn into ash. I wondered if he had a girlfriend and what his name was. I looked forward to the next day with excitement for the first time in a long time. It was a new excitement. One I had never felt before. Maybe he'll think I'm too young, I considered, but I dismissed that thought as soon as it came because I knew I had most likely lived a thousand lives compared to most of the girls in the community. Was this all in my mind, or had he felt it too? I wondered as I swam in anticipation.

The Sparrow thought she may have spotted her mate. A male who stood on the side of a dusty dirt road. One who tightened his muscles and remained fixed in her direction as she slowly flew by. Living inside a new nesting community would take some getting used to, but she had migrated to many unfamiliar nests before. The Sparrow's first impression of this foreign world was one of safety. One of open land and quiet people. One she thought she could endure until she matured enough to fly away to her very own nest.

Chapter Twenty One
The Community

Eventually, I made my way over to my desk. I sat down before flipping the hourglass upside down and watched as drops of sand fell to the bottom. I flashed back to the beach by Sandy's house and told myself, 'One day, I will dip my toes into the sand again.' I then fingered through the bible. The pages looked ordinary. There weren't any pictures of men holding magical scepters or of women being stoned to death as I had imagined there might be. David never hid his beliefs regarding a woman's place, "*God's chain of command*" seemed his mantra. According to him, God's chain of command placed God at the top of a pyramid ("the head"), then the Prophet, then men, followed by women and tailed by children at the base. So, I imagined wild fear-inducing illustrations might have been depicted throughout the bible, which was intentionally placed on my desk and positioned as part of a plot to convince me of the "truth" as David knew it.

The sounds of a bird chirping pulled me out of my bible gazing zone. I remembered Britches and couldn't believe I had spaced saying 'hello' to the little guy upon my arrival. There in a far corner of the kitchen, he sat perched in his lovely cage. The cage Uncle George and Aunt Betty bought for me. Wanda and David had cared for him while I was away. Something about his needs being met during my absence aroused a tender feeling inside me. He didn't seem to have changed at all. It was refreshing to see my blue and yellow pal, who wore the outline of black pants. The sight of him conjured up fond memories of my aunt and uncle. Seeing Britches evoked wonder in me. Would I ever see or hear from them again? I longed to look into my uncle's sniper eyes and smell my aunt's fancy perfume again. I missed feeling their shield of protection and hearing their voices. I wanted to be a recipient of Aunt Betty's coaching tips once again and to hear her say things like, "Shoot for the stars by aiming for an education." I loved them so much. Our distance and time apart hadn't quenched my thirst to see them.

"Magdala. Are you here?" I heard David ask. Oh god, I thought. I realized I would need to decide to address Wanda as Magdala or Mom while in their home. I had respectfully referred to her as "mom" since our reunion, but I grit my teeth each time I did. It was even hard to say it when I was so desperate that I picked up the phone and called her. I still could not help but wonder why I felt more comfortable living with someone who sold me for groceries than with Sandy and Teri?

I knew what Teri was about and what he was potentially capable of, but I also knew what Wanda was capable of. No wool covered my eyes when it came to either of them. However, Teri had only tried to touch me one time. He never tried again physically again, as I had feared. There was a chance he would have with Cassandra gone, but I didn't even know if what I thought was going on between them really was. Wanda had put me through so much pain, but I felt a sense of ease with her, Vicki, and Lee. Why? I couldn't understand myself. I wondered how I could be more comfortable with a person who had beaten me, left me alone, and stolen every attempt I made to discover a talent by slaughtering my drawings and poetry with her words. She not only hurt me but allowed others to do so, yet here I was.

I admitted to myself that I simply didn't feel right being a foreigner in a different culture called someone else's home. I realized I did not possess the capacity to relax even when the environment around me was safer, like at Sophia's and Kris's. My incapacity to emotionally rest inside a home other than Wanda's haunted me, and I hated myself for it. I was strong, but I couldn't kill that beast. Not yet. I could and had endured her beatings and intolerance for me as far back as I could recall, so there was no nuclear unit learning curve with her. The discomfort of being a stranger in someone's home was worse and, in many ways, more painful than my familiarity with evil. There was an unexplainable gravitational pull inside my mind which acted as a tycoon who had a say regarding my birth bond.

Later that night, I slept better than expected in my small bedroom. I loved the weight of the handmade quilt, and it smelled safe, and the fact that my door was locked added a layer to my comfort. The carpenter boy's eyes were the last picture I saw that night. While butterflies stroked their soft wings under my skin and happy jitters tapped danced inside my heart, I drifted into a deep sleep covered in peace.

The next morning, I woke up like it was Easter Sunday. David was the first person I saw. "Well, good morning, sunshine." Never had I sensed there wasn't something off about him, but he was certainly making his best efforts to befriend me. "David, do you not work anymore?" I asked him. "I work here now. There's a lot of work to be done on this property, and I help things run smoothly around here. We all do our part to serve each other and God. Your mother uses her seamstress skills, and Vicki and Lee help in the areas they can. I don't need to be a machinist for worldly people who are on the wide road leading to destruction when I'm needed here." A question concerning my grandparents' teachings floated through my mind. They had taught me Jesus commanded us to love and serve all people. That would have included the people in the world and outside of the community, but I decided not to embark on the subject and to save my questions for a later day.

I brushed my thick, wavy strawberry blonde hair as I looked at its length. It hadn't made its way back to my waist since I butchered it off with kitchen shears, it rested just below my breast now. I saw a pink container of mascara and decided to try it. Wanda had worn that forever. I couldn't believe how long my eyelashes looked with them on and how my eyes popped three shades lighter. I looked in the mirror, and once again, I saw someone new beaming back at me. I was no longer that little girl who whacked off my hair while looking into a dingy, blackened motel mirror. I was no longer the girl who had considered running those kitchen shears through my ears or dreamed of using them to slit my wrists.

I was now a young woman who carried a flame of fire inside my eyes instead of daze, dread, and sorrow. My heart was no longer innocently open for entry and hungry for Wanda's love. The walls around my heart had turned into a fortress, and its brokenness lay buried within its stone fortifications. I no longer craved death but desired life. However, like Britches, I was still inside a cage, but I knew when the day came on when the door would open, I would fly high and rise into the updrafts. Flying alone if I must, like an eagle, but I vowed to myself that I would soar above it all one day.

"You're not seriously going to wear that, are you?" Vicki caught me in the hallway and inquired as her eyes widened and her mouth turned into an oval. I suddenly wanted to smack the smug look off her face, but emotionally pulled back. "What's wrong with what I'm wearing, Vicki?" "We don't wear shorts like that here. God expects us to be modest. You look like a Jezebel." She asserted. *Who are you, and where the hell did my little sister go?* I contemplated. It was at that moment I wondered if she had remembered. Had she remembered life before Uncle George? Had she remembered me protecting her by climbing on top of a man to relieve him when I was eight years old to keep him from her? Or was this it? Had she only known Mommy as Magdala?

I realized there was a chance Vicki and Lee would never remember the things I knew. Torn by what I might decide to say or not say one day if that be the case. Would I share with them that there lived an evil witch named Wicked Wanda before Mommy Magdala came along? Would I share with them what "Magdala" the "Strong tower," had done before she became a "Child of God," or would I let our shared history rot away and decompose into another skeleton?

The time had come. It was time to meet members of the community. If it weren't for the carpenter boy, I would have easily insisted on passing, and BECAUSE of the carpenter boy, I also considered insisting on passing. We walked into a hall filled with people. There were so many members. *Holy moly, what is this place?* People stopped us as we walked to find chairs, and not even one failed to say my name with a loving smile across their face. How did all these people know my name? Had Wanda found another man with some sort of clout just inside a different world? Did one of the leaders send out a memorandum that announced little ole me was coming?

I glanced around the crowd as we continued to our seats in hopes of seeing the carpenter boy. I didn't see him. There were groups of people closer to my age divided by what looked like age groups and gender, but he wasn't there. His face, the only face that mattered, was missing from the crowd. I greeted those I was introduced to, but my mind, soul, and spirit were roaming around the room. I had never experienced apprehensiveness like this before. A one-sided intensity played like passionate music in the air until its sound wave moved through another carrier, causing two heads to turn towards each other. Our eyes locked. His dark penetrating stare locked me to him for what felt like an eternity until I chose to reveal my own strength by turning away. The resulting sound wave constructively increased the amplitude of a force that existed between us. I glanced back again, and he did so at the same time before we both looked away. A tuning fork was at play. I would know him. I was on pins and needles but was bustling inside to know him. *What is his name? Aaron, Jason, Jebediah*? I wondered, but I'd have to wait until the right time to learn his name. I also wondered if he already knew my name since it appeared everyone else seemed to.

The movie was lame, and everyone sat with their families. No cliques of girls sat in a row together. A large majority of the females were plain looking but pretty. Compared to the length of my hair, most looked like they had horsetails. The whole experience was peculiar, but I didn't feel threatened by these people. I felt safe with them even though I hid my reserved right to believe they DID NOT know the "truth" and WOULD NOT be the "only people to survive the war of Armageddon."

When the movie ended, everyone clapped and got up rather quickly while a leader announced from the stage that all the women and children of school age would need to meet in the hall on the following Monday to get set up for school. Magdala's demeanor around the church members was comparable to her demeanor when she had been around Uncle George. She was quiet and lacked smiles, unlike most of the women who glowed and flowed throughout the room with big Texan-like smiles, many were surrounded by little children. Yet, Magdala stayed by David's side, wearing her sober expression. *Did she hate herself inside there?* I wanted to know. I could possibly forgive her if she did, *but if she didn't, how could I ever forgive her?*

I felt him again before I saw him. He was standing in the back with the guys he had been with before. Closer to the exit doors. Something fierce and mighty rose inside my chest. It was something strong I couldn't name because I hadn't met it before. As I walked past him, I was aware others were watching our visual embrace, but we didn't seem to care because our gaze held on. Our energies rubbed up against each other as I passed him and stayed connected until I reached the door.

"Hey, Brother David," I heard someone call out. When I turned around, I saw him. The carpenter boy was walking towards us. Walking towards me. "Hey, there, Adam," David responded as they shook hands before sharing a brief man hug. *Adam, his name is Adam...*David formed the beginnings of what would be a brief conversation by asking him how a recent supply run into town went. Adam conveyed a few details before gesturing my way. He put out his hand, "Jade?" he questioned with a nod. I reached out and shook his hand, *Adam?* I answered with a similar nod. When our eyes met, and our hands touched, a twin flame was ignited. A flame powerful enough to keep its own fire burning.

The Sparrow had matured faster than the other birds due to her environment. Spring had passed for the Sparrow, but inside her heart, mating season was just beginning.

Chapter Twenty Two
Knee Deep

My ears tuned into a conversation between David and Magdala when I heard them mention Adam on the short drive back to our house. A drive that would have been about a 15-minute walk, "Adam's doing well since his return." David said. "He's a good kid. I've always liked him." Magdala responded. I wanted so badly to inquire about him, to learn more about who Adam was, but I couldn't bring myself to ask at that moment. I was still learning and gauging this new mom of mine, Magdala. I also assumed any inquisition about a person of the opposite sex might trigger one of David's hour-long preaches, or, worse, they might pick up on my attraction to him.

The following Monday, we were back at "The Hall." Magdala, Vicki, Lee and me. Excitement rose inside me the closer we got to the building. I wondered if Adam was there. Had he thought of me? I wondered where on the property he lived and thought about his leaving the community at one point and questioned why. I realized we had only shared a few glances, a nod, and a handshake, but my mind continued to be drawn to him.

I considered that maybe all the "brothers" were nice like he had been, and he had simply been cordial. Perhaps it was just me, and he would think I was strange if he learned of my thoughts. After all, he did have a work connection to David and had referred to him as "Brother." I considered the possibility Adam was trying to forge a bond with David because his father had been ex-communicated and forced to leave the community.

The hall was filled with women and children by the time we arrived. Only a couple of male leaders were in the room. It was surprisingly organized compared to what could have been complete chaos in another setting. There were women "teachers" who took the lead that morning, but not when it came to a prayer that was given from the stage. I had learned back at home we shared for a time with my uncle, that in this religion, women were not allowed to pray over a group with a man present, and when they did pray for someone other than themselves, they had to wear a covering over their head. Magdala was too reserved and self-conscious when her body wasn't flooded with white powder or liquid courage, so I had never seen her be the one to pray. I did, however, hear her pray with Vicki and Lee, but she never came into my room and tried to pray with me.

Several of the women called "teachers" stood near designated cafeteria-type tables divided for different grades and gender. The boys would be taught in separate groups from the girls, but women would be their home school instructors. Magdala was not a volunteer, which did not come as a shock to me, but she was there. At least for that first day. She still wasn't a soft mom full of fuzzy warm words, but I could see she showed more interest in us and seemed to want to ensure we got into the right groups.

I stood in a line for 9th-grade females before learning my group number. Making my way over to a table marked **"#12 The Esther's."** I sat down with a folder that was given to me at the check-in table. Girls sat around me, and although friendly glances were exchanged, no one said hello. It was apparent they knew one another. I was used to going to new schools, but this was a new type of different for me. As I sat among "The Esther's," I couldn't shake the feeling that when they looked at me, they saw the wrong sort of mark on my forehead.

"Hello, I'm sister Rebekah for those of you who don't know me. I will be your teacher this semester, likely until summer's harvest." Sister Rebekah had the softest voice I think I had ever heard spoken. She looked and sounded like a little songbird. Even the way she moved her hands fanned femininity. I also had the sneaking suspension; I was the only one new at that table, so I found her greeting kind.

Sister Rebekah asked us to pull out our schedules before proceeding to go over what our studies would look like for the first semester. We would be doing most of the subjects I was accustomed to. However, she mentioned how we were "blessed" to have "real food and not the food of the world." As she proceeded, I translated what she was saying to mean, we would not be allowed to look at or read worldly literature." Startled by the sting of my cuticle, I noticed I had caused it to bleed. Questions were popping off inside my mind.

The carpenter boy Adam no longer entertained my thoughts. Was this a legal school? What has Wanda done to me now? How will I ever go to college if this school is made up of crap? My head spun as waves of nausea swam through my stomach. I had settled on what this might all look like, but now I wondered if the schoolwork I did would matter to the outside world. I had to go to school. The very thing I once dreaded had become my only way out. Was I in a Catch-22?

Everyone who sat at that table most likely already thought I was a "Bad association." What might they think if I question the authenticity of our studies or their structure? I finally raised my hand. "Yes, Jade?" "Ms. Rebekah," I began, in which she was quick to correct me by saying, "Sister Rebekah." "I'm sorry," I said. "Sister Rebekah, do we have a principal here?" I don't know why that was the question I chose to ask, but it was the one that came out of my mouth. "Jade, God is our principal." She replied.

No, I told myself. *No. This cannot be legal. I will not let Wanda steal any more of my education.* She will have to drive me to a school in town or even to a legal home school program, but I have to go to a school that counts. I searched the room to find her. But she was gone. *She had already freakin left.* I stood up and told Sister Rebekah I had to use the bathroom to rinse the blood from my hand, in which I did before making my way past a "brother" who I told I had to go home for "personal reasons." I would not be a part of it. I knew enough to understand states required us to learn certain materials, and never heard of a school not having a principal.

I headed down the narrow dusty road. My first real walk alone since I had arrived. The sweat on the back of my neck grabbed a hold of my hair, soaking it within seconds of walking outside the building. It was so humid. I felt like I was sucking in the dirt. *Who doesn't wear shorts in weather like this?* I wanted to scream. *God, I hate my life.* I said to myself. *Now what?* I questioned. I heard a car's motor from behind and headed closer to the edge of the road to allow it to pass. I wondered if someone from the hall was coming to get me. I didn't turn around. I just faced forward and kept walking.

Darn it! The vehicle was slowing down. "Hey, Jade, right? I looked over my left shoulder to see Adam talking to me through a passenger window as he slowly drove a small truck next to me. "You, okay?" he asked. I don't know what came over me at that moment, but I indignantly stopped and sharply responded, "Actually, no! I'm not. I'm not okay. I can't do this." "What exactly can't you do?" he questioned with a charming white smile. "I can't go to a school that is not really a school. I mean, what is the point of that?" "Uh, well, some people think it's important to learn to read and write." His words were playful, and his attempts to cheer me up inviting, but I felt like I was in a no-win situation again. "I want more than that!" I exclaimed. "Ya, and what exactly is it you want, Miss Jade?" "Aren't I like your sister or something?" I asked while giving him a thumbs-up.

I was so irritated by the realization that I was being enrolled in a fake school. Some off the government grid school, all the excitement I felt when I thought about Adam was gone. I was about to unload my wrath on him. A person who grew up here. Who might report me to the leaders who would want to arrange some sort of exorcism on me by the end of the day?

"You wouldn't understand but thank you for stopping." I just wanted him to leave so I could figure out what I was going to do. "Jade, stop walking. Try me." "Isn't it a sin or something for you to be talking to me alone right now?" I asked. "Would you like to get in and give me a chance to understand and maybe even help you?" "Get in? We can't be alone inside a truck. I know that much." "Hey, it's up to you," he said as he came to a stop and pushed the passenger door open. "Adam, I don't want to get you into trouble." "Do I look afraid?"

I slid into his truck and shut the door behind me. "People can see us." "If you're that worried about it, duck down," he laughed. "Do you trust me?" "I don't know you freakin know you!" Angry Jade had risen, and cutesy play games were no longer on my radar.

Adam drove past the church and around the pond until he came to an area in which he parked. The bush covered the area. He explained there were a few trails leading to swimming holes, but no one should be there since the school was in session. "Why aren't you in school" shifting one foot in front of the other as I followed him. "Oh, I finished that a last year." "How old are you?" "I'm 19, and you are the same age as my younger sister." "That's creepy," slipped out. "How so?" "Never mind," I said as we made our way through shrubs.

We came to the water's edge. I could tell people had been there before. The embankment was flat, and grass covered the dirt. Shrubs hollowed out a covering which provided shade for my upper body while I was able to make one of my daydreams come true by kicking off my shoes and putting my legs into the water up to my knees. How I loved the feeling of cool water on a hot day. It wasn't only the feeling but the smells. The fragrances of the earth, the grass, and the clean scent of the water. I couldn't see the bottom. It was too cloudy, but the pond felt and smelled alive instead of stagnant and murky. I swayed my legs back and forth in the water while the anger inside me wilted away.

"You want to talk about it?" Adam asked. "About what?" "What caused you to leave school today?" "It's not a real school. It's pointless." "Why do you think that?" He looked puzzled. "There's no principal. There are no "Worldly books." "How can that be a real school?" "Jade" "Ya" "You're cute when you're mad." I let out a giggle as I realized my chest was beginning to rise and fall. "It is legal. In this state, people have the right to educate their kids without the state's interference. It's even legal for parents to create a report card and grade them. There is a protocol in place, but it's completely legal here. That's why a lot of believers move here. I mean, when you really think about it, why should the Government dictate the education of someone's child? A child who doesn't belong to them."

"But I want to go to college, how will that work?" "College, hmmm, that's a word you rarely hear around here. Why?" "Adam, I have to go to college, or I will never be free." "Ah," he said as he placed his hand on my cheek. "Who told you college is the way to freedom?" "Jade, that's not the truth. Freedom comes from above and lives on the inside. It's not something you can buy or even earn. Freedom is a gift." Our eyes connected. His gaze melted my fears away as he inched forward.

"Jade, can I kiss you?" I nodded my head, "Yes." Butterflies fluttered inside my tummy as others made their soft swings caressed my body. I wanted him to kiss me. This was different. He was different. I closed my eyes and felt his lips press against mine. I felt his strength and his tenderness bundled into one. He opened his arms and motioned for me to come closer to him. I rested my head on his chest as he wrapped his arms around me and held me. He just held me. "It's going to be okay, Jade. Everything is going to be okay." he repeated while stroking the back of my hair.

The Sparrow found a safe place to rest. She would have to decide if she would stay in her new resting place or would she find a way to do what she needed to do in order to fly free one day?

Chapter Twenty Three
Adam

I succumbed and surrendered to make the best of community life. There was an urge inside of me that had become a monster greater than any other desire. The desire to know Adam and stay near him outweighed my craving for education and the ability to one day care for myself. I chose to learn the ways of life, as he knew it. I didn't know if I could ever be close to Wanda, Magdala, or my mom, but I would do my best to "honor" her. To get to know David and to get to know God.

When Adam gently kissed me that day, I felt what I knew could only be labeled as love. There by the water's edge, Adam wanted only a kiss and to comfort me. My innocence had been stolen a long time before then, and I might have allowed him to go further, but he didn't try. He only kissed me again before telling me he'd better get me home and that a search party was likely out looking for me.

When we neared what was now my house, I saw how right Adam had been by the group of men gathered around David. Once again, I found myself wanting to flee. I wanted to get out of his truck and run fast down the dirt road and out of the exit gate, but Adam assured me he had it covered and told me to wait in the truck. The windows were rolled down so I could hear everything.

Look who I found wandering near the swimming hole, Adam said as he approached the group. Since Adam had instructed me to stay inside his truck, soaked in humiliation, I remained stuck to the seat. I had run off many times before, but no one had ever looked for me. I always did an independent walk of shame back to Wanda's door when I was with her.

I expected to see the men, especially David, pull Adam aside and rebuke him somehow, but handshakes were exchanged instead of hostility. After a gratitude-filled departure, David and Adam approached me. Adam opened the door while casting one last lure at me with a seductive look as I exited his truck. David patted Adam on the back before the guy I just had the most intimate moment of my life with turned his back to me, got into his truck, and drove away with only a nod to David.

"Jade, young lady, we need to talk. Would you like to walk with me, or would you like to come inside and have something to drink?" David asked. Is there a third option, I wondered, like an alien abduction? I told David I was dying for a drink of cold water, so tagging behind him, we landed at the kitchen table. David asked me if Adam had been good to me and if he had "Respected Me." In which, I told him he had. I explained I had left the hall because the school didn't sound right or real, but that Adam had explained it was a legal program. I felt comfortable enough with David to share that education was important to me and that it had never been important to my parents. I told him I wanted to go to college and have a career someday like my aunt had acquired against adversity. How her father had believed in her even when he had been challenged by men in their culture who believed differently.

"Oh, you dear child. Adam is correct. Freedom is a gift from God through His son Jesus Christ. Earning a wage will not give you freedom. It would provide you with a way to support yourself if you chose to remain unmarried." David continued by sharing with me how he had served in the military, and that was where he had been taught to be a machinist. He said he was thankful for his skills and the ability his skills gave him to earn a wage and to create the important parts he had made in his life. Yet, it was only when he met Jesus that he found freedom.

"The young man you were with today fell into deceit at one point and believed the same thing you do. Did he share that with you?" David asked. I lifted my eyebrows and deferred my words with a head nod, implying Adam had not shared that with me but imploring I would like David to. "Adam's father left the community because he questioned the prophet and whether the Day of Judgment was near. He grew concerned about his son not having higher education or a skill that would support him outside our community. He fell short because of his lack of faith. He did not believe in God's promise to provide for His children and started to doubt what was coming to the world. Well, unfortunately,

Adam followed his father. He was gone for nearly two years. He fell into immorality, drank, and even got a few tattoos, but like the prodigal son, he returned to his family and, more importantly, turned away from his sin. Adam no longer speaks to his earthly father because God opened his eyes to the truth. You have been told many lies, Jade, probably more than Adam. When I met your mother, she was filled with lies from the devil and a religious spirit, but I sent that spirit away, and God delivered her from the lies she had been burdened with. If you choose to give your life to your eternal Father and our Lord and Savior, you too can be delivered from your burdens and receive the freedom you desire. If not, your mother has shared with me there is a family you can visit if you want to leave. She believes Sandy and Teri would invite you back into their home. We are not forcing you to stay here, Jade, but we need you to understand that there are rules here. What you need to decide is if you are willing to follow them or not. It's up to you."

 Those words were easy for David to spew out, but living them was a different story. Had he ever lived with strangers and been an outsider in someone's home? Maybe he had been. I didn't know, but I wasn't going to disrespect him at that moment with my thoughts, nor was I going to leave. An anchor attached to my soul had dug deep into the land the community rested upon. Not because of Magdala, David, Vicki, or Lee. Not even due to my discomfort of being an outcast in another family's home but due to a soul tie that had fastened my body to the community. I had observed two sides of Adam: one that prioritized passion over rules, and another that sought validation from the men in the community. Over the following school year, my mom and I began to make small talk. After my time at the pond, she did comment on how I was already causing trouble for her, but I was so exhausted after my lengthy talk with David that her words had little impact on me. I began to feel closest to her during church on Wednesday evenings and Sundays mostly because she seemed to draw closer to me before and after services revealing her need for a companion. The fact that she had not fully opened up to the members who lived in the community about her previous life. The fact that she was still hiding a part of her history from her "brothers" and sisters" and from David did not escape my notice. I also gravitated towards her during those times because I couldn't find a friend there besides Adam. I loved that there were people of all races, and I did want a girlfriend like Annie had been to me, but the females remained distant from me. Sister Rebekah was kind to me, and I did my best to excel academically. I also started to pay attention to the sermons at church and was assigned to help some of the older women harvest wild plants and herbs to make medicines with. I enjoyed being in that space with them, and working with herbs reminded me of my Grandma Georgia.

 A desire to know more about God also grew inside me. I sat at my desk and did as David had requested. I flipped my hourglass over, read scriptures, and later discussed them with him. Vicki and Lee were always eager to pitch in during our Bible discussions, and my mom was there most of the time if she wasn't cooking. However, she did not venture out to preach to me nor to make any comments. It amazed me how a woman who had run drugs, pointed a gun at a person who cut her off when we were driving down the freeway, and who would take off with her 3 kids and bald tires to towns covered in snow now bowed down to a man in the name of religion. I couldn't understand it. While we were at home, the home Uncle George arranged for us to live in, I believed she was faking her redemption after she met David at a house church. But now, a few years later, she had become even more submissive. I still caught glimpses of evil in her from time to time by the tightness of her jaw and by the darkness that would cover the green landscape of her eyes, but she contained those glimpses well as I had done before. I could spot masking from a mile away, thanks to her. I had buried myself, my hurt, my secrets. I imagined what she hid was something far more wicked than I could comprehend, but I could finally relate to my mom in one way—we were both buried underneath dead bones.

 Over that year, I became fond of the structure I now lived in. Something about it helped the fear of the unknown leave me. Our life was penciled out on paper. Adam and I found ways to see each other. We had to conceal our meetings under the guise of a duty of some sort or of the need to be alone with God, but when we were at church or family gatherings, he watched me out of the corner of his eyes. When I looked his way, he looked mine. He tied a promise bracelet on my wrist and told me I belonged to him. He said that we would be married and that he would approach David and the prophet for approval when the time was right. We grew close, and our passion intensified. Our hidden moments included me sharing some of my darkest secrets with him while he shared some of his. He taught me what a man's tender touch felt like, and I was introduced to the pleasure of a welcomed touch. I felt safe with him and wanted to share everything with him. All of me for all of him.

The Sparrow found her mate and discovered her first love. She decided to nest with him at all costs. She left behind her hopes and dreams for a safe nesting place.

Chapter Twenty Four
Diving In

I took the plunge in a lukewarm inflatable hot tub. Members clapped like ducks flapping the water off their backs when I emerged. I got baptized. I believed it was the right thing to do. I also wanted to be proper marriage material for Adam. Afterward, David and a handful of leaders sealed the deal by giving me a "spiritual name." Me becoming a "Child of God" warranted such a prophetic declaration.

"Jericho," David announced from the platform. "Our Mighty God brought down the walls of her heart like he tore down the walls of Jericho. He plucked her from the world and turned everything the devil meant to harm her into good, into strengths, into powerful anointing, and calls. He is building new walls, a hedge of protection around her." David then handed me a certificate of baptism which was issued to someone else. I didn't especially like the name they chose, but I didn't dislike the meaning either. After all, I had never seen myself as a precious stone.

I did a headfirst dive and swam to the deepest depths of the community I could reach. I conformed to many of their ways. Some I liked, some I didn't. I jumped off the deep end because I wanted to be with Adam. I had decided to stay and learn his ways. I wanted to marry him. At least, I thought I did. I dwelled in daydreams about him while allowing bible stories to take me to faraway places like Rome, Greece, and Israel. I was able to connect dots and draw lines between what my grandparents taught me and what I was learning. Theological differences emerged from time to time. However, by large, the greatest contradiction being end time prophecy. One story ended with an apocalypse referred to as "Armageddon."

Grandma Georgia believed that one. The "Children of God" also believed in the war of Armageddon, with the slight difference that they would be the only ones who survived the great apocalypse while the rest of the world went to hell. Grandma Drucilla and Grandpa Pay believed there would be a large revival of people who would get the bride of Christ ready before He returned. The "Children of God" also believed there would be a great revival, but that revival would be made up of individuals who converted. I connected dots and drew lines where I could, but I was playing *Dots and Boxes* with religion. Who'd win that game? Regardless, there were some things I sincerely liked and admired about the community.

There was a different kind of peace there. It was a space where ethnicities came together as one big family, even with the chatter and the backbiting. When it came down to it, they were there for each other. I think due to our penciled-out schedules, I learned to relax a little. The rug, which had been pulled out from underneath me so many times before, had been put on pause. Yet, I was still in the waiting for the mark on my forehead to change. It was easy to spot. A mark of the beast which stood between me and close friendships with other females. I was family, but still potentially "bad association." An egg that was one part whole and one part rotten. Adam was my only friend and so much more.

I fell in love with him. It may have been adolescent lust on my part, but it didn't matter. If it was lust or love which tied our souls together, who knew, but the knot was weaved tightly. Concern over the nature of our relationship arose while whispers hissed from all four corners. Adam's sister Emili had a heyday stirring the pot. Emili Addison hated me for reasons only God knew. She did her best to act sweet as pie but could not fool me with her skills. I saw the molded apples beneath her Dutch Crunch front. I had been teased before, I had seen looks that turned away too quickly, and I had swum with sharks.

I would have liked my new rival to have liked me, but her lack of love wasn't a deal breaker for me, nor did she scare me. She was a spoiled brat and bordered on psychotic. I thought it was weird for someone to be so fixated on their brother and who they did or didn't like. Meanwhile, Adam and I chose to practice purity. We decided to save ourselves until we married and did "what was right" in the eyes of God. However, that was after several encounters which went way too far. I clung to the promise bracelet he gave me on days we couldn't see each other. Duties ate most of our time. His being greater than mine. Leaving little room for us to sneak off to meet, but we found our way. Every encounter with Adam left me feeling like I had just gone for a swim inside a poet's mind. He was gentle but strong. He had a fire in him like me. Even in his obedience, he walked like a soldier. He was romantic, and he was beautiful. Adam, in his entirety, represented the word perfect.

Late nights teetered between fantasies of what life would be like when we were unleashed and me pleading with God to give me a clean heart. I also had conversations with God concerning my anatomy. Was it okay? He didn't speak back, but I begged him to heal any damaged parts of me and to "please, Lord, make me whole again." Adam had touched me, caressed my most private areas, and didn't seem alarmed by anything. He appeared to be as pleased as I was during those times. However, I was still tormented by the big question, '*Was I a virgin?*' With everything that had happened, I believed I wasn't. How could I be? I wanted to be for myself and for him, but I thought that dividing factor had split a long time ago. I had experienced too much pain for my body not to be broken in places that should have remained preserved. My right to choose was cut from me. I shared many of my secrets with Adam, but what happened in the basement stayed in the basement. He knew I had been sexually abused, but he didn't know the extent of it. Neither did he know that Mommy Magdala had been my madam for a season.

A madam of sorts that I needed to forgive. A commandment that now sat on my doorstep. It would be the death of me if I didn't forgive her. My inability to know what forgiveness looked like grew into a monster who wouldn't stop reminding me of it. He also enjoyed shaming me about the things I had done, seen, and experienced. What sucked the most was his ability to overpower me. I felt guilty a lot during those years. The Monster screamed, "You are commanded to forgive because Jesus forgave you. Who are you to not forgive the sins of others? Jesus was flogged for you to even have a chance at eternal life in Paradise." I would shout back the reasons why my case was different. I was not met with even an ounce of sympathy or compassion in the space between my ears. "If you don't forgive, you will die in the battle of Armageddon. God forgave you and your transgressions. Are you better than God?" Sometimes I told the Monster to go jump in the lake and that if God was love, He would understand that I could never be close to my mom.

During academic seasons I did my studies but lost my attachment to the idea that education was an outlet for freedom. However, with each "A" I earned, I jumped up and down like I was on a trampoline while roaring with excitement only no one would have noticed because I hid the fact that my heart was bouncing like crazy, and my lungs were screaming at a pitch no one could hear.

"Happy Birthday to you, Happy Birthday to you," sang Adam to me on my sixteenth birthday. My feet were covered in straw. Bales of hay surrounded us. Adam handed me a small box. The heat caused my cheeks to turn the same shade as the barn. *This is it. The day has finally arrived.* "Adam, you didn't." I covered my mouth, but my hand wasn't wide enough to cover my smile. "Well, open it, silly," he said, looking at me with calling eyes. I wanted to tell him how much I loved him. I wanted to scream "YES" from the rooftops. Only shouting anything would have most likely caused the Calvary to come running.

I pictured a small diamond placed beautifully on a dainty gold band. "Jade, you're killing me, open it already." I carefully grabbed the corner, opening it, I squealed with excitement. Folds of yellow legal pad paper ballooned out of the box. The paper popped out like a rabbit in a magician's top hat. *'Paper, where's my ring.' I wondered.* Oh, he must be asking me to marry him in a fun way. Bewildered, I covered my mouth again, acting surprised as could be. I smoothed out the yellow-lined folds and frantically searched for the words "Marry Me," but like a ghost, they were invisible.

I slowly read his words:

Dearest My Love,

You are the love of my life and my soulmate. You are my everything. I'm asking the Prophet today. Happy Birthday, my beautiful blonde blossom.

Forever us,

Adam Jeremy Addison.

"The Prophet? How about me?" I was instantly sent into a spiral by his letter. I was pissed. I knew. I knew he would have to ask for permission, but I always imagined he would ask me first. I threw his letter at him. "Jade, what's going on?" Adam involuntarily flexed like he was turning into the Incredible Hulk. "Call me crazy, but I thought you'd ask me first," I screamed. My concern others might hear was obliterated. Adam's brown eyes sank down into his innermost darkest space. I had never seen him look so angry but was too ticked to care. I had grown in the community's ways and developed a reverence for God, but all my conditioning blew out the window at that moment.

"Go Marry The Fucking Prophet," I screamed as I picked up his letter and tore it into pieces just like Wanda had done to the portrait I drew. I stormed out of the barn leaving a yellow trail behind me. Steam shot out of my ears. Likened to an angry bull who just spotted red, my instinct was to charge, get away, take a rake, stab it into a wall, and hit something. Once again, thoughts of grabbing a bag and disappearing spoke to me. A convincing dialog that failed me many times and only served as a reminder that I was still inside a cage, just like Britches.

In my mind, Adam was strong. His proposal was weak for a guy who had been like a jaguar on the prowl since I arrived. I didn't like how Adam played by the rules when he wanted to and, at other times, ignored them. Especially when it came to me, he needed to be all in or get lost. I needed his love for me to be stronger than his desire to please people and even God. However, the terror of my actions attacked me before I approached my front door. 'Oh *my god, I said the word "fuck." I talked badly about the Prophet and what God expects of us. I can't believe I just did that. I'm a hypocrite too. Why couldn't I have been nicer to Adam? Why did I get so mad? It's a sin to get angry and to cuss. What the hell is wrong with me?* I attempted to counter those thoughts with one tall question —*Where's Adam?* Was he still sitting inside the barn because he wasn't behind me?

Adam was my anchor to that community. Not that I had many other options, but he passed through my concrete dam and was permitted to swim inside me. Then he nailed himself there. God slid in as well in some ways, but it was different. I would realize later that God held my broken pieces together. He might have torn down my walls, but He fastened the remains together and sealed the leaks because He knew it wasn't safe to remove my fortress completely. Not yet.

It was harvesting season. I enjoyed spending time with the older "healers" and considered sharing with a few of them what was happening between me and Adam. My heart felt like it had been bulldozed over. I needed someone. The sisters taught me how to make salves, poultices, tinctures, soaps, and so much more. Could they teach me how to deal with this? After all, they weren't total sticks in the mud like some of the others. They enjoyed bantering back and forth with snide clever comments. There was a one-upper in the group who would usually end a sarcastic skit before a new one would begin. I quietly and carefully mixed lye and water while listening to the sisters. Even in that process, I was reminded of Adam. The way the water activated the lye. The element of danger to the mix and how it heated up so quickly when it came together. The fumes were killing me slowly.

I thought about how I didn't even get to say goodbye to Grandma Drucilla when she died from a heart attack after Uncle Al fell off his ten-speed bike into a ditch and choked on his vomit. I was sad when I learned of their passing, but a feeling of deep sorrow for Grandpa Pay stung me. I wanted to be there with him. He loved my Grandma enough to endure her three rebellious sons for years. I never heard him refer to her as anything other than "honey." I missed him. My dad had been so rude to Grandpa Pay, but he was there at his funeral. I wanted to be there for him, but at the same time, I didn't want to leave Adam.

Adam didn't want me to travel either. He told me he was afraid I wouldn't come back. I thought about them for a few days. Their deaths conjured up a lot of memories. Including some of my dad, but greater was my grief for my grandpa than the rest of the gang. I did feel bad for Uncle Al and wondered why Uncle Pete wasn't the one strangled in a ditch by his vomit.

A few weeks passed, and there was still no sign of Adam. Every knock at the front door felt like a gorilla beating on my chest, but I was disappointed each time. *Where is he?* I had been too much. I disrespected him and might have even hit him if he tried to touch me, and I think he knew it. I showed him a side of me he had only seen glimpses of before.

"I know about Adam's request," David said while sticking his finger inside his earlobe to scratch it. He cleared his throat before continuing to tell me Adam had submitted a request for my hand in marriage, but Adam was already promised to another. He has been for some time. An arrangement was made known to him shortly after he returned and repented. I watched David's mouth move, but the piercing pressure inside my ears silenced his words.

Adam knew he was promised to someone else this whole time? I felt sick. This was worse than anything I had ever experienced. I believed him. I gave my heart to him. I trusted him. I couldn't wrap my mind around what David was telling me. His words were surreal. I curled into a fetal position and cried until my soul became a desert wasteland. I was experiencing an emotional drought, starved by thirst, and Adam was the only one who could quench it. I had to see him. I had to hear it from him. I wouldn't take this lying down. I would get up again. I would apologize for how I had treated him. I would tell him he didn't have to marry someone else. I would convince him that God wouldn't want him to marry someone he didn't love.

The Sparrow's nest was saturated like a punctured waterbed by her tears. But then the straw ran dry, and every drop dissipated. Leaving the Sparrow thirsty and dehydrated. Leaving her stranded in her desert wasteland. She needed to find her mate. He and only he could take her to a place where her thirst could be cured.

Chapter Twenty Five
Shunned

I was determined to find Adam, but the consumption of grief filled my body like a cocktail loaded to the rim. I was the robot version of myself again. I was paralyzed by reality. David's words were on endless replay. Adam had known all along. He was just like everyone else, a liar. The burn of it was a blistering blanket, but I still wanted him.

"Jadey Pooh." Wanda sat on the edge of my bed. "You know, a lot of them think they're better than us. They think they're better than me because they don't have a past." "Mom, are you trying to comfort me in some weird way?" I asked. "You've never comforted me a day in my life, and that's what you have to say?" Our eyes squared off. "He's another guy. The girl he's supposed to marry is ugly enough to make a freight train take a dirt road. And you, you were my ugly duckling, but you turned out to be prettier than the rest of them. Of course, Adam will want the new pretty little fish in the pond, but you both know the commandments."

My voluptuous hourglass made its way into my hand within a flat second. "I should beat you upside the head with this, you fucking bitch!" I screamed. Thump, Thump, Thump, my heart wanted to break through my ribcage and grab her throat. "It's you. You destroyed my life! I hate you. I will always hate you, you greedy evil slut!" I tightened my hand around the hourglass and hammered it into the wall. I slammed it repeatedly until Wanda put her hands on my shoulders. I turned just in time to see her fly backward and land on the floor. "Don't you ever touch me again!" The Calvary came running, banging their shields, and before I knew I had a man on every side of me holding onto some part of my body. I resisted until all I had to fight with was the air flowing in and out of my nostrils.

"Calm down. Just calm down," David whispered through grit teeth as if he was silencing a demon. For the first time in my life, I could see a fear in Wanda's eyes that was placed there by me. "I want to talk to Adam!" I screamed. "He's gone. He's gone. He left." David said. A bomb exploded...shell-shocked, I froze. *He lied, and he left me here alone*? I jerked my way out of the circle and sat in my desk chair. Pushing my bible aside, I laid my head on my forearms. I had pushed my mom. Adam was gone. My education was a joke. My dad was dead. Razors glided through my chest until the arrow's fletching's stopped it. The arrow held my torso together while the rest of me was a wooden puppet doll on loose strings. *I could die here now, and it would be better for me. Maybe Jesus would have mercy on me. Lord, let me bleed out. I don't want to do this anymore. I don't want to be here anymore.*

I heard a commotion outside. Everyone had disappeared from my room except for the arrow in my chest. *Here comes the exorcism. Wait, is that Adam?* My chest sucked in the arrow's fletching like a Hoover vacuum on overdrive as I stood to my feet. I heard Adam's voice in the chaos-fueled chorus. I ran to the partially open front door. Grabbing it, I swung in wide. Our eyes locked like magnets; my north grabbed onto his south. The strength between us was large enough to cause my body to move in his direction without thought.

Adam opened the passenger door of his truck, "Jade, get inside," he said as he looked at David and the brothers. Gravity might have pulled me into Adam's truck, but the adrenaline of the best kind brought me back to life. Adam and I looked at each other, and a smile emerged. I turned to see Wanda standing near the front door behind the bobbing heads and smiled as Adam drove away.

Brothers stood in front of the exit gate. To my surprise, they stepped aside and opened it. As we passed, Adam gave them that ever-so-friendly brotherly nod. Then he peeled out and left them with a dust storm as a goodbye gift.

"Get over here," he shouted while grabbing my leg and pulling me close to him. Still a bit shell-shocked. I was at a loss for words. At the same time, adrenaline gave me a gnarly head rush. Forget about butterflies. This was so much better! *He came back for me.* It all started to click. *He left because he was angry. Mad at them. Then he returned despite them to get me. He loves me. He just told them all to go to hell to be with me.* I was undone.

I laid my head on his sweaty arm and didn't mind getting sticky. *Just breathe,* I told myself. Flashes of me pushing

Wanda passed through my mind, and I could see the expression on her face as we drove away. I felt bad about pushing her. The fact that I had thrown her to the floor hurt me. She was my mother, and I had never wanted it to be that way between us. I don't know what came over me, but whatever it was, it was too late to take it back.

Adam drove down the narrow dusty dirt road. I kissed his arm softly. Leaving abruptly wasn't new for me, but it seemed like the older I got, the scarier it became. Shouldn't it have been the other way around? "I thought you left. Why didn't you tell me about Heather?" I asked. "I couldn't. It would have messed things up." He replied. "Messed things up how?" I questioned. Chuckling while tossing his hand up in the air, Adam looked at me, "Jade, does it really matter now?" I laid my head back on his arm. *No, it didn't matter. It didn't matter now.*

"You must be the famous Jade I've been hearing about for the past few weeks. Come on in, young lady." Adam's dad was taller than him, but they resembled each other quite a bit. He was older than I had imagined. He looked like he was in his 60's, maybe even early 70's. But he was handsome, nonetheless. In a Clint Eastwood sort of way, except with dark hair and eyes like Adam. Henry was his name, and to my surprise, Henry had a law degree. A tall Texan attorney who once moved his family to the community. Only to later leave them there. Life looked very different for Adam on this side of the gate.

Henry's main room was covered with mounts. Ranging from white-tailed deer to wild boars. Elegant tannin-stamped concrete floors spread throughout the spacious adobe home. Compared to this, I must have looked as messy as the houses back in the community. Henry was welcoming, but I felt small and dirty. Once again, I only had the clothes on my back. I told Adam I was embarrassed to meet his dad this way. He gave me that seductive smile, pulled me close, and kissed the top of my head. Small and dirty, I might have been standing inside that pristine adobe home, but I was safe and loved in Adam's arms.

I soon learned I did not need to be concerned about material things. Henry was more than generous to me. I didn't want him to see me as some poor girl, and I especially didn't want him to know my past. A man like Henry's had a grace that only extended so far. I was thankful that leaving the community seemed to camouflage everything else. Henry was still bitter because he was excommunicated. I wondered how a man like him ever lived there. It didn't add up. Perhaps even smart, wealthy people with proper education can find themselves inside a symbolic cage of sorts. Henry no longer believed in God. I wondered if it was because the community had hurt him. Nevertheless, he was more than accepting of me and, in many ways, took me underneath his wings almost immediately.

Okay, so here I am. Sixteen, in a beautiful house with the guy I love. Now what? I'm too young to get married to

Adam. I haven't finished high school. I couldn't even drive. My dad was dead, and he couldn't sign any of my papers for anything. Wanda was behind the gate, and I pushed her. Which I still felt terrible for. Not because I regretted it as much as because I didn't want to be one of those who physically harmed their mother no matter what. I tried to apologize, but at the same time, I reminded myself that I didn't hit her and of the times she had brutally beaten me. The times she left me bleeding without even a look of later regret. The times she sent me out the door to school with fat lips and knots all over my head. The times my private areas had taken days to stop burning. *I pushed her, and I felt like crap. Why? I wondered.*

I pushed those thoughts aside and realized I needed to decide what to do. Fortunately for me, Henry liked to help other people solve their problems. He started by gifting me a used Jeep Cherokee. It was a little beat up around the edges, but I loved it! It was mine. Adam taught me to drive, and Henry took me to get my permit and signed the paperwork like he was my father. No one questioned it. No one questioned him. It seemed like everyone knew him everywhere we went in town.

I was able to recover a few items from the community. I didn't go back, but Adam arranged to pick up a few of my belongings. He was told not to return while doing so and was notified that he was excommunicated. In a little suitcase, I found my bible, a letter signed by "Mom & Dad" written in

David's handwriting, my birth certificate, and some clothes I would never wear again. Adam said, "Brothers" stood at the gate to see him out. It wasn't the first time Adam had left, but I could tell he was upset. He loved his mother and siblings, even his rotten little sister. He felt guilty for leaving them. He also had a lot of friends there. Friends he considered to be true brothers in Christ. And while it was true that Adam had left the community before but this time, it would be different. Like me, he had been baptized after his return. Baptism was a game changer. Once baptized, one became an official member of the community and of the greater "Children of God" religion. The gate wasn't a swinging door. Prodigals weren't allowed just to change their minds and return once they were baptized. There was an official excommunication process. It went something like this—six months of shunning. No one and I mean no one except a handful of leaders and the prophet, were allowed to speak to you. If members, even members who shared your DNA, saw you on the street and you said "hello," they kept walking as though you didn't exist. If a person, after that six-month waiting period, wanted to return to the community or to the organization period, the first step would be taken in writing. One would need to draft a letter of intent. The prophet would take the matter to God, and things would proceed from there, or they wouldn't. In the meantime, not a single person who identified as a "Child of God" was allowed to speak to us. This was God's way of disciplining us through his people according to them, and God "only disciplines those He loves." A shunning somehow intended to turn us away from the world and back to them. I wondered if I picked up the phone and called Wanda if she would really hang up on me. For me, it was weird, and it did sting a little, knowing Vicki and Lee were most likely in the audience when they announced my ex-communication. However, the loss was much more painful for Adam. He was strong and loved me and his dad, but the community was his family. I knew part of him wished things could have been different, but we were shunned. Plain and simple. The gate was closed.

The Sparrow's mate found her. She didn't have to search for him after all. For the first time, the Sparrow felt like someone had fought for her and her alone. He cured her thirst and brought her back to health. Afterward, he flew her to a new nest. A nest where he would stand guard over her. A love nest where they could rest

Chapter Twenty Six
Fun In the Sun

Henry surprised Adam and me with tickets to Hawaii. He called it a "Summer Vacation." It was a summer vacation I was more than gracious to take. Things would be changing soon. I was enrolled to begin 10th grade at an Independent High School. The school required one hour of weekly one-on-one time with an instructor and some campus hours for testing. I considered attending a regular High School for a minute, but I felt a knot in my stomach when I thought about it. Compared to when I was younger, only for different reasons. Attending school was optional now. Which, like the knot in my stomach, also correlated to my elementary life. I may have gone to school, but for the most part, no one at home cared about what happened there. The exception being Uncle George and Aunt Betty. They cared; they cared a lot. And believe it or not, David ended up caring as well. David had turned out to be a pretty nice guy. I recalled my concerns of someone creepy lurking inside his cool demeanor, but I had been wrong about him. Even with his irritating ability to turn every topic into one-hour preaching, I knew I would miss him.

I made the call I needed to make to Wanda about my report cards. I had to get a record of completing certain core classes for proper placement. "Hello," Wanda answered. "Mom, it's me." I held my breath briefly, wondering if she would hang up. "Mom, I need my report cards to get placed at school. I'm also sor..." She cut me off before I could finish telling her I was sorry for pushing her. "Go look in your bible," she said before the phone went dead. My report cards were indeed inside my bible. I realized I hadn't opened it since I left. I wanted to believe she placed them there, but more than likely, David had.

I had a few weeks before school started. I couldn't believe Adam, and I would spend some of that time alone in Hawaii. We were stoked, we were inseparable. I had never felt so close to another human before. I was attached to him like Velcro stuck on a wool sweater sleeve. I loved him with all of me. He was my home. I didn't feel like an outsider with him and Henry. In fact, they poured affection on me and treated me like a princess.

Adam made love to me for the first time inside that adobe home. My heart jerked beforehand when I had a spontaneous thought of God. I sometimes wonder if that was God whispering to me. Adam was gentle but strong and defined. He kissed every part of me while we laid naked together on the bed. He didn't rush and was tender about the fact that I was a little bit afraid. The warmth and pressure of his manhood entering me hurt, but soreness became a fervent fever within moments. Entangled like noodles fresh out of the pot, chemicals skyrocketed to euphoric heights. I wanted him. More of him. All of him. Sex wasn't an assault. Not with Adam. I wasn't in the basement anymore.

Afterward, I looked for signs...I browsed Adam's expressions for any indication of disapproval, knowing it hadn't been his first time. It was when I went to the bathroom, and I saw a little bit of blood. There wasn't a lot, but there was some. I wondered if God had answered my prayers and restored me. Then felt bad about having sex, but I convinced myself God would understand. After all, we were engaged. I reminded myself Old Testament law stated engagement was a contract of marriage.

We landed at a relatively small airport on a Hawaiian Island. When we exited the plane, the smell of salt infused with lovely fragrances struck my nostrils. The sun glistened while emerald foliage decorated the landscape. Pine trees waved in the wind, saying, "Aloha and Mahalo for coming." The very air greeted us with a perfect hug of humidity. I was in heaven. Adam had been there before, but years prior.

The first night we danced and drank like the "Worldly" people we had become. Adam had turned 21, which was the legal drinking age there. Knowing the Pacific Ocean surrounded us was exhilarating. I loved everything about it. I felt happy, untouchable. Unfortunately, during our stay on that incredible island, I would see Adam's dark side for the first time.

My hair had grown long again, and I started wearing some makeup. Black mascara and soft pink lipstick, to be precise. I landed at 5'6, weighed 118 pounds, and sported a full C-cup. I looked nothing like my Grandma Drucilla. In fact, I didn't look like anyone I knew. I noticed that guys were checking me out while wearing my white bikini, but that had become relatively common. The glances, I mean. Adam picked up on it, too, and reminded me of how he warned me my bathing suit was too skimpy. He had a simple one-piece in mind, but he liked my bikini and didn't resist grabbing me when I stepped out of the dressing room wearing it. He just didn't appreciate the fact that other guys liked it too.

We were headed back to our room after a full day in the sun and a full day of drinking when we passed a small group of guys. I looked away immediately, but the word "damn girl" echoed from behind me. I felt Adam's rage before I saw it. I was shocked when he stopped and positioned himself to square off with them. Adam may have spent most of his life wrapped in religion, but he wasn't afraid to speak his mind nor fearful of standing up for what he wanted and believed in. From the day he drove me away from the community, he became very protective of me. I learned what the intensity of those initial gazes had been saying when he was free to be fully himself.

"What are you doing?" I asked him. "Let's go. Those guys are stupid. "I told him. Adam grabbed my arm, pulled me close, and said, "If you didn't look like such a damn whore, this wouldn't be happening." I recoiled away from him. Pulling away, I reminded him of how he encouraged me to be free, to which he responded, "And by telling you to be free, you thought I was telling you to act like a slut?" I told him I hadn't done anything wrong and "could care less" about those guys. I loved him.

He wouldn't let it go. His body language warned me to be quiet on our elevator ride up to our floor, but part of me was irritated. When we returned to the room, he slammed a beer, smashed it in his hand, and tossed it into the waste basket. "What is your deal? "You are acting completely ridiculous. I love you; this is crazy." Those were the last words I spoke before Adam used his hand to keep me from speaking another word. He grabbed my throat and slammed me into the wall. "If you loved me, you wouldn't act like a little whore." His eyes went black like Wanda's used to when she was high on meth. My Adam was gone. His eyes weren't his anymore. He dragged me by my hair and straddled me on the bed. His weight pinned me down as I fought to escape from underneath him. That was before he smacked my face. It was a blow that turned into an oscillating fan blade which struck me repeatedly before he covered my mouth to mute my screams. When he was done, he sat on the bed with his head in his hands. I wiped the blood off my mouth and realized my nose was bleeding too. I ran to the bathroom. My already full lips doubled in size, and slivered rips were all over them. Blood dripped from my nostrils. My pink patchy face and neck cried for help. I couldn't believe Adam caused the injuries I saw in the mirror. I couldn't take it in. I couldn't breathe. I was crushed.

During the night, Adam rolled over and wrapped his arms around me. The sting of my lips was small compared to the lacerations inflicted on my soul. My body stiffened in response to his touch, "I'm sorry" he whispered. "I love you." He said. I didn't want him to touch me, but at the same time, his embrace and his words made me hurt a little less inside.

The next day, Adam showed me he was sorry with his wallet and words. I sported sunglasses to shield both the sun and the blue and purple lines across my lower lids. I was hurt. But by the end of the next night, his showering attention blew up memories of the altercation into tiny details while a new picture formed.

My love for the Island was greater than any place I had been to before. The Island, the ocean, and my toes in the sand overrode anything that attempted to ail me. The Island fed any leach that tried to feed off my heart to the fish. On day four, Adam and I were lip-locked like two Angelfish swimming together in the warmth of one of nature's great salty baths. I was sixteen, but I drank what I wanted, and did I ever; especially, after that bad night. I roamed around our room and the resort-like I was a woman of a much older age. Adam spoiled me with gifts and attention, and I spoiled him with my body. It was as though that horrible argument had brought us closer together. Our passion for each other increased. I loved him, and he promised he would never get physical again, and unlike Wanda, Adam was sorry.

The Sparrow, along with her mate, returned to their adobe nest to begin again.

Chapter Twenty Seven
Trapped

Vivian was a burly woman with a gruff voice who finished each sentence with a questioning brow or with a loud, boisterous chuckle. She was also my junior high instructor. I had pep in my step after leaving our first meeting with an arm full of schoolbooks. I was going somewhere. Maybe not physically, but I was in movement. I drove myself to and from our meetings and small group testing hours while Henry pressed Adam to enroll in a junior college. Henry's smaller of his two dogs barked for Adam to in the "least study to get a damn contractor's license."

Meanwhile, Adam started going to a local bar with a group of guys. Abandoned, not old enough to go with him, I was reminded of when Wanda left me alone inside the basement motel. I hated it when he went to the bar. He also started sleeping in and sitting around during the day with his head stuck inside a computer game. I questioned why Henry gave Adam money but, out of respect, kept my curiosity to myself. Henry also paid for my auto insurance and gave me money for gas, but he did it in the name of "doing something" with my life.

Adam's jealousy and rage increased as time went on. An orchestra of violent events would be the unfolding of us. There were holes in our bathroom and bedroom, and one even made it into the hallway. He was good at throwing a little drywall over them, but each remained a memory of an ugly altercation. While sitting on the toilet one day, I looked up at one of the holes and just stared. Strangely, it reminded me of the white ink that covered Wanda's racist tattoos. It wasn't just Adam who was physical and jealous. At first, I was "madder than a wet hen" as Grandma Georgia might have put it. When he stepped inside our room after his first known visit to the bar, I smacked him a good one right upside the head when he walked into our room after exchanging a few vulgar words. It didn't take me long to figure out Adam would always win in the end. The harder I fought, the worse it ended for me. After a while, I stopped fighting back. Nervousness debunked boldness to a lower rank.

I took Henry up on an offer to sleep in a spare room one night while Adam was at the bar. Henry played a part in our pattern and knew the routine. He'd hear sex or fighting; he didn't care to listen to either one. However, he noticed screams from Adam's blows outweighed my moans and started to intervene. The spare room was unlocked, and I was glad to take it. Not even so much to protect myself but to demonstrate to Adam I could be fine without him. The truth being I trembled at the thought of what I would do or where I would live if we didn't work out. I considered a women's shelter, but then I remembered my age and realized it would most likely be a foster home for me.

We always made up, me and Adam. The pattern became nearly set in stone. An unseen, almost supernatural water wheel powered our relationship, and I was at a loss for how to stop it. The only break from my reality were the hours I spent with my head buried in books. Vivian complemented my understanding of figurative language and appreciated my love for poetry. In some strange way, I wanted to please her. It felt good when she gave me kudos.

Unfortunately, as much as I loved Adam, things worsened. He and Henry were at odds, and Adam just wouldn't "do a damn thing" for himself, as Henry put it. Adam's spunk and seductive cute smiles, kind words, and humor diminished as the year went on. While cradling me one evening, he asked me if I had missed my family. I shared with him that I missed Vicki and Lee, but I knew they were safe and didn't miss anyone too much. "What about you?" I asked. "I don't know. Sometimes I guess." He responded. I felt guilty at that moment and wanted to make his grieved vibes I was picking up on to go away, "Maybe you can go see them." I suggested knowing darn well he couldn't. *Am I the reason Adam can't see his mom, siblings, and friends?*

I knew deep in my heart he wasn't only missing them but his place in the community. If it weren't for me, he would still be there. Had I become a Venus fly trap who was paying for my sins with blunts and blows? Did Adam secretly blame me for being excommunicated? Like the night Adam came home to find me missing from our bed. He immediately began screaming my name throughout the house, which woke me and Henry. When he found the room with the locked knob, he pounded on the door, nearly breaking it down before Henry raised his voice and demanded Adam walk away. The following day I had to be on campus for testing. I sprang up early, sporting a commotion hangover but was thrilled to get out and go to campus. I made a few friends there. No one I did anything with, but it was nice to have subtle conversations with people other than Adam and Henry.

Adam usually slept until noon after a night at the bar, so I wasn't overly concerned about slapping into him before I high-tailed it out of there. However, a little on edge, I jumped inside my Jeep, eager to go, but when I turned the key, my beloved Jeep made a solitary click. It wouldn't start, and Henry was gone. I had two choices. I could skip testing and lock myself inside the spare room or wake the monster. Neither thrilled me.

"Adam, Adam, wake up" Shaking him, he opened his eyes. "Adam, my Jeep won't start." Sitting up higher on his pillow, he asked me how that was his problem. "I need to go in for testing today. I can't miss this!" "Well, you can forget about that." Adam said while rolling over and turning his back to me. "What do you mean?" "You're not going there anymore." "Yes, I am. I have to go to school." "No, you don't. That's a big fucking lie, and you know it." "I'm sorry about last night. I was just upset you went out. Please help me get to school. I promised Vivian I would be there."

I pleaded with him to take me to school or, at the least, take a peek at my Jeep before he answered me by grabbing my throat. Adam clenched his teeth together and pulled my face close to his, "I will take you, and I will watch you get out of my truck, and I will walk you through those fucking heathen school doors" he said as his splattered spit moistened my makeup. My eyes filled with water as Adam jumped up and yelled, "Go wash that shit off your face." Adam pushed one of the campus doors open and motioned for me to pass through. On the outside, looking in, he may have seemed to be a gentleman, even prince-like, but I knew better. I could feel Adam. A haunting superpower. True to his word, he shadowed his tiny pet mouse right into the testing room, where he gave Vivian that gentleman-like nod before he unleashed me. My brain hurt. The puzzle pieces of my life I had been building scattered apart. It was hard to focus, knowing my neck still had Adam's handprints around it.

"Jade" Vivian called. "Come see me in my office, would ya for a minute when you're finished?" I concurred with a nod of my own. "Talk to me." Vivian said as she pulled up a chair. "About what?" I asked. "About your hot dog of a boyfriend, that's what" she replied with an "I see it, Affirm it" kind of a squint. "You in some kind of trouble? I can help you." "No, I'm fine. I'm totally fine." I lied through my teeth, knowing Ms. Vivian wasn't buying it. "You know, sweetheart" she said. "What people don't work out, they'll act out." With that, she excused me while looking down at her desk. Humiliation covered me on my way out as I recalled her eyes looking at my neck. I knew she knew.

My attachment to Adam was the strongest I had ever had to a single soul in this world, but daydreams of life without him started to play through my mind. Not after the choking, the name calling, or even the beatings—but on the day I learned Adam dismantled my Jeep to prevent me from driving to school. When we got home, he popped the hood, tied some loose wires, jumped in the driver's seat, and turned the engine over. A cage door was closing and locking, and Dr. Jekyll-Mr. Hyde held the key.

I suggested a counselor, but "Children of God" members didn't believe in shrinks. After undoing my Jeep wires, Adam turned to take my keys. Hiding my keys so he didn't take them became part of my daily routine. I decided to get a job. I wanted to save money in case I needed to leave. I was hired on the spot at a fine dining restaurant as a hostess. Ms. Vivian signed a form permitting me to work up to 25 hours per week. I would earn my own money to escape if need be. My Jeep became a potential place of lodging. I had slept in cars before with Wanda. I think I even slept in a car with my dad once. *I could do it now by myself if I needed to,* I told myself. Sometimes I felt like I hated Adam, then he would pick me up, throw me over his shoulder, and take me to the bedroom. The strength of his love and the tenderness he showered upon me was unmatched. That was my Adam, the Adam I loved. However, like Drunk Gary, he changed when he drank and seemed determined to live a life-sucking resource from his parents.

Adam started to show up at my work. He would sit at the bar and watch my reflection through the bar's back-splashed mirror while tossing back one beer after another. Eventually, his tempered glares at me and toward the guest drove management to ask him not to return. He yelled, "Fuck off!" on his way out, hushing the customers who chatted over a candlelit meal. I acted as though I didn't know him and continued to work, but inside, I trembled. I was a pet mouse who kept returning to a trap that would painfully catch me before releasing me to do it all over again. I liked the food even though I knew getting close to it would hurt me in the end. The temptation, the love of the lure, and the smells overpowered the hurt. But the pain of the trap began to outweigh my cravings.

It was a flaming hot Saturday in late spring. I had to be at work at 3:30 pm to help open for the dinner crowd, the only crowd when I realized my keys were gone. "Have you seen my keys?" I asked Adam. His response shook me, "I'm driving you to work." "*What? Why?*" He pulled my body to his, pressed himself against me, and kissed the top of my head, "Is there a problem with me wanting to drive my wife to work?" He said before he kissed the top of my head again. I was hit by a hot wire. Something wasn't adding up. My sensory system screamed, "Don't go!" But I ignored my faithful friend and went with him.

That Saturday, I wore my hair in two long braids mostly to combat humidity-induced frizz, but I liked the look. Adorned in my polyester uniform and light tan pantyhose, we headed out the door. Everything seemed fine until Adam drove past the restaurant. A traffic jam of rapid heartbeats, shallow breathing, and partial paralysis collided. "You passed the restaurant! Where are we going? Turn around." His gaze remained fixed on the road ahead, "you really thought I was going to take you there?" he asked with a sinister breath. "WHERE are we going?" I yelled. Adam pulled behind a building full of offices. Signs read "Attorney at Law" and "CPA Services." Offices commonly void of staff on a late Saturday afternoon.

I reached for the doorknob when Adam stopped his truck, but he was quicker than me. An anchor hooked itself around my neck from the backside. With his other hand, he slapped down the lock. I fought to get out, but the anchor held me there. Trapped inside the cab of Mr. Hyde's truck. I registered a painful amount of heat blowing through the vents before realizing Adam had turned his heater up full blast in 98-degree weather with a humidity level of 62.

"STOP. I CAN'T BREATHE! STOP! I LOVE YOU. PLEASE, let Me Go." I pleaded and made sad attempts to free myself, but it was pointless. My uniform stuck to my body, my precious pantyhose wet and itchy. With beads of sweat running down his face from the raging heat, he yelled, "You love me? Ya, you love me so much you fuck other guys? You need a lesson. You need to learn what it means to be a submissive wife." "I'm not your wife" I fired back before he grabbed my hair and slammed my face into the dashboard, "You little whore, you are a fucking Jezebel!" "Stop, Adam, stop. I'm sorry." I cried as blood and sweat flowed from my face. The inhalation of heat and the absence of air made my head dizzy and full of despair. I pleaded with him to stop as he reached over, pulled up the lock, pulled the doorknob back, pushed open the door, and threw me out. "Trash, you're trash Jade Cadell." He slammed the door and peeled out, leaving me lying on top of the hot asphalt.

Ripped nylons, missing rubber bands, messy hair, and a tear-stained- face were all I had when he drove away. I was late. If I walked to work, I would be even later even though it wasn't far, but I couldn't go to work. I looked like I was just in a car accident. I couldn't walk into work like that. I found a dry ditch alongside a fence. My legs stretched, feet touching the bottom, and with my back to the world, I. spilled a thousand sobs into that ditch when I heard the words, "Who are you?" My world swirled with memories starting with an image of me singing "Wheels on the Bus" at preschool. Then shot through the blackness of voids to the smile of Grandpa Pay.

To me, being unable to run away while inside the basement. Then Grandma Georgia appeared, standing by her clothesline underneath the walnut trees. The vision merged into a memory of Uncle George sitting across from me on the lower bunk. I heard his words, "You're tough as nails. This is a dog-eat-dog world. Decide what you want and never quit on yourself." I snapped out of the vision, "*This will be the last time he hits me. He will never touch me again.*" I didn't know how I would leave or where I would go, but I would get away from him.

The Sparrow's mate turned into a different creature. He was no longer the beautiful male bird who fought for her. Now he fought her. He mobbed everything she gathered. It was time for the Sparrow to fly in search of a safe nest again, but she wasn't alone. She had a helper who had returned to remind her of who she was. He would be by her side while in flight.

Chapter Twenty Eight
On the Road Again

I never went back to the fine dining restaurant that had been kind enough to give me my first job on the spot. I made my way to Henry's office, overheated and bloodied. The house was too far away, and my purse was still inside Adam's truck. He left me without a dime to my name. Adam never came back. He left me on the asphalt like I was a used wrapper that flew out the window. A piece of trash some good citizen might pick up and throw away. I walked into Henry's office, thankful to find he was alone. Grateful he spent more hours there than at home. He dropped his pen when I walked through the door. His pen wasn't the only thing that dropped. The bottom of his mouth looked like it was running after the pen that fell on his desk. Henry gasped in shock, like he had just witnessed a murder. I told him everything. Through tears and lots of ugly crying, I spilled my guts right there on his office floor.

"Jade, I've grown to love ya, kiddo, and I love you enough to tell you to get as far away from my son as possible. Do you have anyone we can call? Any family other than your mother?" I shared with Henry that Grandpa Pay still lived in the town I originally came from and that I believed he still lived in the same house, but I didn't know for sure. "I don't even know his phone number." I told Henry. "You know his name, don't ya?" Henry replied with his raspy voice and slightly tilted grin. "Yes, I know his name and the town he lives in." Henry turned to a new machine in his office, called a computer, and told me with a little time and help from his good friend, he believed he could get Grandpa Pay's phone number and address. "In the meantime, let's get you home, girly."

I felt like that small mouse crawling inside Henry's adobe home, tattered and torn. Yet even though I felt small and broken, my cravings for the bait waiting inside Adam's trap lost appeal. I knew the allure of Adam's love bombing was a façade. A ticking time bomb waiting to crush me again. I entered the spare room with Henry shadowing closely behind me. I didn't want Adam's comfort this time or his deep sorrowful kisses. Something inside me had changed. His comfort would no longer appease me until the next explosion. I wanted to get away from him. My eyes were opened to the fact that I was in a relationship with someone who was a cross between my mom and my dad.

That day I became an outsider inside Henry and Adam's home. I was just another drifter passing through. I wanted to leave, and right now wasn't soon enough. With my mind roaming once again, I desperately searched for a new dream to cling onto.

The next morning, I and Adam's makeup dance started with a soft knock on the door. "Jade, open up. I just want to talk. Come on. Open the door" begged the asshole who left me on the asphalt. The craving to feel him wrap his beautiful arms around me, the need to hear him tell me he was sorry and how much he loved me, laid buried in the ditch underneath my tears. I ignored tugs on my heartstrings by tuning into my thoughts. I told my heart we couldn't play anymore. The music had stopped. The dance was ending. It was as if my heart and mind were split in two, but I was determined to let my mind lead me. I no longer trusted my heart. I hardly trusted my mind but believed it might serve me a little better than the organ that had been weakened by lost hopes and dreams of being loved. Truly and fully loved.

Should I tango with him long enough to put him and ease so I can safely sneak off without him dismantling my Jeep or taking my keys? What if he destroys my Jeep completely? I pondered the practicalities of leaving, knowing Adam would do anything within his power to keep me from going. I needed to be smart. I needed to wait for Henry's help. I needed to see Vivian before I left and make sure Grandpa Pay was still alive. I opened the door. I felt sick to my stomach as Adam reached out his arms and pulled me into him. His embrace warranted a good healthy visit to the Porcelain God, but for some damn reason, a cry swelled inside my throat until I released it with uncontrollable sobs. "Hey, hey…I'm so sorry. Baby, hey listen, my love, I wouldn't have gotten so darn upset if it wasn't for those jerks you work with. I asked you to stop working there. It's me and you, remember?" I nodded my head up and down before allowing my wet cheeks to take refuge on his chest.

Henry moved faster than I expected. He contacted Grandpa Pay, and my sweet Grandpa said I was more than welcome. Henry mapped out directions and stops along the way. He even prepaid a night's stay at two different Hotel rooms along the way and ensured I had my roadside assistance card. Additionally, he gave me $500 for my travel costs. At about $1.17 a gallon, I would have more than enough to make it to Grandpa Pay's.

I kissed Adam farewell before leaving for school. I had given my body to him the night before to throw him off the scent of my escape. *One more time.* I told myself. *One more time.* I hated him, but part of me still loved him. However, I was just waiting for the moment in which I would leave, regardless of my wavering emotions. I slowly rotated my clothing in preparation for my big leave. Every piece of clothing remained neatly folded. To his untrained eye, my shuffling around would look normal. I gathered my toiletries in the same manner. Everything bundled closely together waited in stillness to be tossed into my bag.

Vivian was kind enough to print out my school records. She even wrote me a little note about how much she appreciated my student conduct and how she would miss my "pop-ins." I said goodbye to her with a smile. She lifted a brow and nodded. She knew, I knew, she knew. I could see it in her eyes. No words were needed. "Goodbye, Miss Jade. Keep going and don't look back" were her last words. I liked

Ms. Vivian. Even when her boisterous laughs sounded like an unhinged hyena with a dry throat. I liked her.

Henry told Adam he wanted to take him to look at new trucks while I pretended to be sick. I hugged Adam and Henry goodbye, but only Henry knew he would most likely never see me again. My heart hurt. I hated that it hurt, but the truth is, it did. It took all the courage I had to get inside my Jeep. I was more afraid to face the unknowingness of the journey which awaited me than expected. I kept telling myself *he will never hit me again. No one will ever hit me again. Nor will anyone ever keep me from going to school or work.* I had the key in my hand now. I could and would decide whether to stay or go from here on out. No one would ever lock me inside a cage again.

The drive felt like it would never end. My feet hurt, and there was nothing fun about it except for little sparks of excitement when I thought about being free. My emotions on that drive were like waves breaking over and over again. They ranged from joy to mourning and back again. Little whispers resembling the Helper's voice came and went also. I prayed and thanked God for being with me. I thanked him for the spurts of adrenaline that shot through my jugular, encouraging me to keep going. I thanked him for the reminders that freedom was almost close enough to touch. I'm not sure if it was him who sat in my passenger's seat on that drive, but to this day, I believe it was.

It was as if someone was trying to lift a weighted blanket off me during that dreadful drive. Memories of Grandpa Pay came and went, and when they came, I felt just a little bit lighter. I looked forward to seeing him. His arms were safe. He wasn't wired with hidden explosives. I wondered if Uncle Pete still lived at my grandparents' house. I was ready for the little leprechaun if that was the case. I would tell Grandpa Pay everything he had done to me. I would even say it in front of him. My Grandpa would believe me. I knew he would believe me. Memories of acorns soaking in pots on my grandparent's kitchen floor came to mind. I smiled as I saw my little fist clenched onto a handkerchief that was tied to my grandpa's belt buckle as we hunted for Indian Soap to cure my poison oak and that smile. The smile that sparkled in his eyes warmed my heart, even in my memories. *Would he even recognize me?* I wondered.

Without GPS to guide me and only a paper map to lead me, I was pretty proud of myself when I saw a sign notifying me— I was 15 miles away from the town I was headed to. About 15 minutes away from my grandparents' house. The place of my birth. *I made it! I freakin made it!*

The Sparrow flew north alone, but was she? There was something about the way the wind blew that carried her. She embarked on a journey to freedom, but that freedom would begin back at one of the first nests she lived in. A nest that was tattered and broken like she was after the storms of her life. She would collect fresh weeds and new branches. She would line her grandparents' house with her feathers until the old became new. Until the smelly flesh that clung to dead bones decomposed completely.

Chapter Twenty Nine
Dead Bones Come to Life

I jumped off the Interstate, crossed over the bridge, drove down the zigzagged road, passed the big red barn, and into my grandparent's driveway. There he sat j, just like in the old days. He was sitting on the front porch on the same dented-up metal chair. My grandpa slowly stood up when he saw me. I threw my door open and ran to him with joy, relief, and a heart full of aches. My grandpa wrapped his thin arms around me, and I once again allowed my wet cheeks to take refuge on someone's chest. Only it wasn't Adam's chest this time; it was my grandpa's. I was more than relieved to discover Uncle Pete had died right there in the living room on that old vintage sofa that had once doubled as my bed and was no longer sharing the same space of this place we call Earth. There was nothing inside me that was torn about that.

Everything looked exactly as I had remembered. Only it had aged like the rest of us. Layers of dust covered every nook and cranny, but the orange shag carpets, the Tiffany look-alike lamps, and even my dad's old royal recliner looked like it hadn't been moved an inch. However, Grandpa Pay hired someone from his church to paint a fresh layer of lilac-colored paint on the walls in my dad's old bedroom. His queen-size bed was gone, and in its place was a twin-size bed with a white head board. W, which led me to wonder if that had been the place. Had my dad let out his last breath in the room that would now become mine? Was it here, underneath a light purple ceiling, that my dad had written his last words?

I knew he had taken his life inside my grandparent's house, but I guess at the time, perhaps I preferred to imagine he had done it camped out in the backyard. Later I learned it was indeed there inside the room that became mine that he penned his final goodbyes. So many lives were lost inside that one little three-bedroom house. My Grandpa Pay had somehow outlived them all. The kind one, the nice one.

It took a lot of elbow grease over the following two years for me and my grandpa to eradicate the haunting skeletons that remained inside that house. Everyone's clothes still hung inside their closets, including my dad's, were still hanging inside their closet. Dolls I played with as a toddler still sat tucked away inside a box on my grandma's side of the closet under her clothes. Pictures, letters, and, yep, you might have guessed it even, faded pages of the nasty girly magazines remained.

We spent months deciding what items would stay, which were worthy of donating, and what would go to the dump. Together, me and my grandpa swam through dead bones. One day while sitting on new baseboards while we waited for the installation of the new carpet, I reflected on all the drunken fights of the nights I was afraid Uncle Pete would visit me. Of the times, I had hidden behind the blinds that hung above the slider. I also remembered beautiful Titania and some other pretty girls my dad had dated.

Slowly the old amber ashtrays, the smell of cigarette smoke, and the stench smell of soured wine faded away. The entryway into the crawl space was sealed and covered by a new carpet. Grandpa Pay and I worked side-by-side. We watched the evening news together and even went to church on Sundays. During some of those workdays, Grandpa Pay shared with me some things I had never been told. He said one day, "You know? That Grandma Georgia never liked that mom of yours much. Boy, she could be a mean one to that little girl. I always felt sad for that one, your mom." I had somehow failed to understand the richness of history held. I hadn't realized how my grandpa would become a wealth of time-held information, how he had been there too, living in that small community that housed the families of the laborers and contractors working on constructing a large new dam. The reason both sets of my grandparents had migrated to that small town, to begin with. The town in which my parents would first meet when they were small children.

Grandpa Pay told me how my mom stuttered and hardly spoke when he first met her. He told me that my mom's dad, a coworker of my Grandpa Pay's and my biological grandpa's, told him that she was never the same after she witnessed the accidental shooting of her sister at the age of 3. How she had been covered in her blood and left in the dirt while everyone scrambled to get help. How her eldest brother, my Uncle George, was sent away and blamed for the months that followed. Months which kept my Grandma Georgia far away in a hospital somewhere with my aunt. "She was sure a pretty little girl, but boy, oh boy, she was a lonely, shy one." Said Grandpa Pay.

I knew my mom had been married off when she was only 14 years old and had my sister Diana soon after, but I didn't know how sad she had been as a small child. Grandpa Pay continued to share stories with me about her that melted my hate away and broke me in a new way. I didn't really know Wanda. I never got the chance to know her because she, too, had been robbed of her innocence. I wondered what kept her locked up inside the community while I was being set free. What is it that releases some while others remain in captivity?

I ached at the images that formed inside my mind of my mom sitting as a little girl covered in her sister's blood, sitting in the dirt all alone. Losing her ability to speak until she was five and the ability to play, love, and be loved. The images of my Grandma Georgia nursing and loving my aunt while my mom was left with a speech impediment and old used garments to wear to school. How she was teased and taunted by the other children with no one left to protect her. How the only attention she ever really received was from men because she ended up being beautiful despite it all. How that attention would repeatedly sour, leaving her without the affection she so desperately desired.

He told me, my biological grandpa, although they were best friends, had a terrible drinking problem. How he had witnessed him tie my dad to a tree in the backyard and lash him "until his legs buckled right out from underneath him." My Grandpa Pay had never been one to gossip or talk trash, so I knew he had a goal when he shared these stories with me. I knew his heart, and I knew he was trying to help me understand what led to my parents being who they were. I knew he was also trying to lead me into a place of forgiveness, which he didn't hide. Grandpa Pay simply was not a loud pressing person. He patiently waited to deliver drops of information to me at the right time. Making sure I was in a place to receive what he was giving before he did so. Like the day he shared with me, he believed my dad purposefully left 101 dollar bills inside his wallet to remind my mom and me of how much the three of us had enjoyed watching 101 Dalmatians together. Something I hadn't even recalled doing.

A nice lady from my grandpa's native clinic helped us file for my grandpa to be my legal guardian shortly after I arrived. She even helped my grandpa fill out the paperwork so he could receive my survivor benefits, which he put into a savings account for me each month. I also continued my journey with an independent study program and worked in the restaurant field. I got another job as a hostess, leading to training as a busser cleaning tables. I liked that better because I earned tips. It was a dirtier job, and I didn't get to look as cute, but it was well worth it. I didn't have to work, but I liked to. My dream of attending college returned despite fearing I would not be accepted to a decent university, and even if I did, how would I ever make that happen financially?

I sometimes thought about Adam in those days after I first arrived at my grandparents' house. I had deep lows, which involved me wondering if he was already entangled with another female. I wondered how he responded when he saw I was gone and if his heart had hurt like mine. I would learn years later that Adam returned to the community and ended up marrying a girl who had been raised there and had a son. I was glad to hear it. He was different than me. He thrived in the grips of organized religion, whereas I felt suppressed.

I walked the line and stayed close to my grandpa over those years, besides one silly night when I decided to go out with a guy from work. He was older than me. A pattern that would continue. My interest in older men, that is. I'm not talking a hundred years older, just a few. Guys my age seemed too young to grasp me. I let go of my restraints and got smashed with him at his apartment, only to wake up the next morning on his bed. I woke up to one of my legs reared out in a splits-like position. I had thankfully fallen asleep with my nylons on, which was a hopeful indicator that I didn't have sex with the guy. However, one nylon leg was shut inside his bathroom door while the other was still tightly secured to my body, causing my tan pantyhose to stretch across the guy's bedroom about four feet and hang in mid-air.

Grandpa Pay had a gentle talk with me when I went home, home to my grandparents' house. By the time I arrived, I had already decided it was a mistake. I wanted a different life. I didn't want to give myself over to years of drinking and blackouts. One day during the summer in which I turned 17 years old, Grandpa's church was holding a baptism gathering down at the lake. I drove him and was captivated by the Pastor's sermon. His church was different than the churches I had been to before. It was even different than the church my grandpa had attended with my grandma. People wore jeans and T-shirts if they wanted to, and the Pastors talked more about love than fear. I sat still and focused on the grass while something moved in my heart. Tears rolled down my face as I was drenched in love, a love I had never known. I began to cry from my belly. A downpour that cleared out my soul. When the Pastor invited anyone who was moved by the spirit to respond, I stood up. I wanted to walk into that water and be made new. This time it wasn't for Adam. It wasn't because I didn't want to die in Armageddon or to appease a single person. It was because I was walking toward love.

When I emerged from the water, I walked out wearing a new gown that was white as snow. Although I would never obtain perfection on this planet, I did find freedom.

The Sparrow's helper taught her how to love by loving her deeply. He taught her that freedom is only found through forgiveness, grace, and a fight to choose differently. He introduced her to what she would later understand to be her very own personal power. The power to choose. He revealed to the sparrow he had been there every step of the way. That he was the one who held her and mended her together when the arrow wounded her. He shared with her that there were many arrows sent by the black cloud to destroy her, but how he had shielded her. Arrows unbeknownst to her.

The Sparrow's dear loved one with eyes that sparkled with a smile would sell the nest she returned to and would send her away with some of the proceeds. The Sparrow would fly to a Hawaiian island to nest at a university where she would learn how to help younger sparrows who battled challenges of their own. She would commit her life's work to helping younger birds. She promised herself that she would forever be a cover for fledglings who had in some way been left uncovered. The two birds she loved dearly who had migrated to Saudi Arabia returned in time to attend her graduation from the university. The bird with the sparkle in his eyes flew to a nest inside a residential community where he was loved and cared for. The Sparrow's mother later died in a hospital bed with the Sparrow sitting right by her side.

National Child Abuse Hotline: 1-800-422-4453 (4 A Child).

Epilogue

Wanda's story is the second of this three-part series (Forsaken). Imagine a young girl of three years old sleeping on old board floors with only a coat to cover her in the middle of winter in the backcountry of Arkansas. A mother far away from home, a father far from her, even though he slept inside the same broken-down cabin.

- *The Arrow and The Sparrow — Never forsaken.*
- *Forsaken— The girl inside the cabin.*

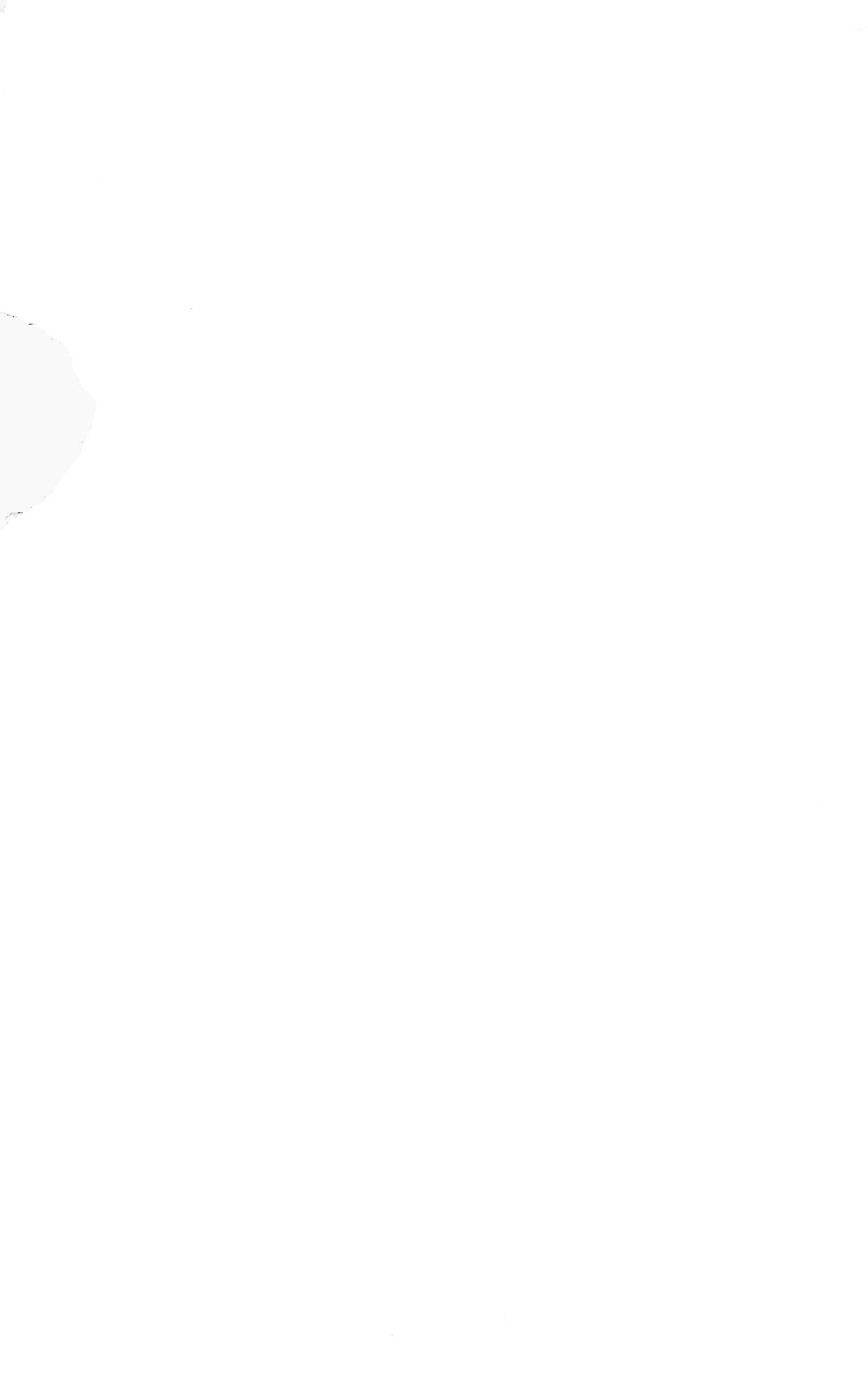

Made in the USA
Columbia, SC
26 November 2023

267d8dad-e56a-441b-8b4d-fd86ec7ba0aeR01